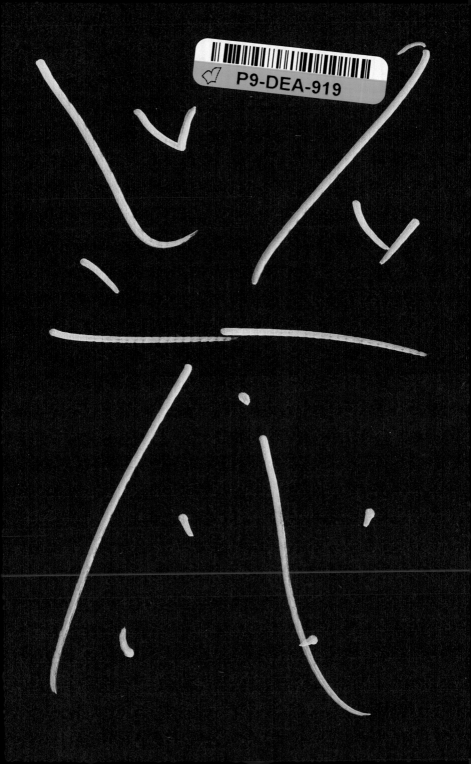

THE DIFFICULTY

OF BEING A DOG

2/12/01

To Ann and Bob —

--- ENJOY

Dad

THE DIFFICULTY

OF BEING A DOG

ROGER GRENIER

Translated by Alice Kaplan

THE UNIVERSITY OF CHICAGO PRESS
CHICAGO & LONDON

ROGER GRENIER is the author of more than thirty books, including novels, short stories, literary essays, an award-winning study of Chekhov, and a study of Camus, *Albert Camus soleil et ombre.* His novel *Another November* appeared in ALICE KAPLAN's translation in 1998. Alice Kaplan, author of *French Lessons: A Memoir* (University of Chicago Press, 1993), is professor of Romance studies and literature at Duke University.

The University of Chicago Press, Chicago 60637
The University of Chicago Press Ltd., London
© 2000 by The University of Chicago
All rights reserved. Published 2000
Printed in the United States of America
09 08 07 06 05 04 03 02 01 00   1 2 3 4 5
ISBN 0-226-30827-8 (cloth)

Originally published in Paris as *Les larmes d'Ulysse,* © Éditions Gallimard, 1998.

⊗The paper used in this publication meets the minimum requirements of the American National Standard for Information Science—Permanence of Paper for Printed Library Materials, ANSI Z39.48-1992

Contents

Preface

Many dogs are named Ulysses. But Ulysses' own dog was named Argos. He waited for his master in less comfortable surroundings than Penelope's. When the ever prudent King of Ithaca finally set foot on his island, he disguised himself with Athena's help. And still Argos recognized him.

> Now with his master gone he lay there, castaway,
> on piles of dung from mules and cattle, heaps collecting
> out before the gates till Ulysses' serving-men
> could cart it off to manure the king's estates.
>
> Infested with ticks, half-dead from neglect,
> here lay the hound, old Argos.
> But the moment he sensed Ulysses standing by
> he thumped his tail, nuzzling low, and his ears dropped,
> though he had no strength to drag himself an inch
> toward his master. Ulysses glanced to the side
> and flicked away a tear . . .

During Ulysses' long exile, Poseidon had persecuted the Greek hero with the vindictive spirit for which the gods are known. Poseidon made Ulysses weep. But now that the traveler was home, it was his old dog who had the power to make him shed a tear.

An Enigma

A few years ago, whenever a tourist visited Paul Valéry's famous oceanside cemetery at Sète and asked the caretaker to show him the location of Paul Valéry's tombstone, the caretaker would wake up his dog and give the command, "Valéry!" Whereupon the dog, all on its own, would lead the tourist to the poet's grave.

A French minister of culture—what business was it of his?—decided that the procedure was not respectful and forbade the dog to serve as a guide for these literary pilgrimages.

Yet I know of a very pretty dog portrait sketched by Paul Valéry himself.

When I'm in the presence of a dog, I always ask myself a lot of questions. I may be naive, but I'm in good company, for Paul Valéry himself shared my naïveté: "The animal, that inevitable enigma, is the opposite of us in its very likeness."

And Lacan: "Dans animal domestique il y a d'homme." His pun plays on the fact that domestic animals are *man*aged.

The animal is "poor in world," says Heidegger, whereas "the stone is without world" and "man is world-forming." This is Heidegger's detour to the question, "What is world?"

How can such an understanding exist between two species? It seems more miraculous, more precious to me than any relationship among humans. At the same time, what could be easier? You come across a dog. A word, a caress, and it responds with no further ado. It is the mystery of these exchanges that led me to write this book. But I know it will resolve nothing and that dogs will never cease to amaze me.

The Difficulty of Being a Dog

"Animals, which do nothing useless, don't contemplate death," writes Paul Valéry.

They don't contemplate death, but they do get bored, as Sartre pointed out in *The Family Idiot* in a rather strange passage. Sartre and his friends were speaking about a dog in the animal's presence. The dog, understanding that they were talking about him, "was bewildered at not understanding what he understood." Familiarity with people, which Sartre refers to as "culture," becomes in the animal "the pure negation *in itself* of animality . . . , but this renewed questioning, this injection of the human as a denied possibility, is translated by a kind of pleasure—the dog *feels alive, he is bored.*"

Which is more or less what Rivarol had said in his *Preliminary Discourse to a New Dictionary of the French Language:*

> Thus nature and the chance happenings of life furnish animals with signs, which means that the kind and number of such signs are greatly limited. Only humans are capable of furnishing them with artificial and varied signs, which, for the animal, are neither natural nor representative.
>
> When we start to treat animals in this way, an insurmountable hurdle soon arises: we have dragged them far from their own realm without transporting them into ours; and the vast

majority of our signs still express needs they do not have, and ideas of which they cannot conceive.

Roger Martin du Gard underlines "the pitiful need to believe, which we see in the way a dog looks at us."

Writing in *The Double Garden* about Pelléas, a young bulldog he owned that died prematurely, Maurice Maeterlinck is struck by "the overwhelming work that oppresses every brain at the start of life":

> In less than five or six weeks he had to get an image and a satisfactory conception of the universe into his mind and let it take shape within him. Humans, aided by all the knowledge of their elders and brothers and sisters, take thirty or forty years to outline that conception or rather to surround themselves, as if living in a palace made of clouds, with a consciousness of their growing ignorance—while the humble dog has to figure it all out in a few days.

It is an apprenticeship that goes against instinct:

> And how to reconcile all this with other laws, other enigmas, greater and more imperious, which one bears within oneself, within one's instinct, which spring up and develop from one hour to the next, which come from the depths of time and race, invade the blood, the muscles, and the nerves and suddenly assert themselves more irresistibly and more powerfully than pain, the word of the master himself, or the fear of death?

The fear of death—here Maeterlinck contradicts Paul Valéry. I would add one rather unreliable piece of evidence for the sake of anecdote. The playwright Marcel Achard and his wife Juliette had a poodle, Gamin, that was almost as much of a personality on the Paris scene as they were. Gamin met his death by jumping out of the window of their apartment on the rue de Courty. Juliette Achard always claimed it was a suicide.

For Maeterlinck, humankind is tragically alone "on this random planet." Impermeable partitions separate the species from one another. With a single exception: "Amid all the forms of life that surround us, not a single species, except for the dog, has made an alliance with us."

Maeterlinck is wary of the horse, the ass, the sheep, the hen, the cat—a fierce creature that "curses us in its mysterious heart"—and even plants. He is persuaded that if they had a little more intelligence and the necessary weapons, all these life forms would be our undoing.

Considering the living world in its entirety, however, he sees the dog as enjoying a great privilege:

> He is the only living being that has found and recognizes an indubitable, tangible, unexceptionable, and definite god. He knows what to devote the best part of himself to. He knows who it is, above himself, that he gives himself to. He does not have to seek a perfect, superior and infinite power in the darkness, amid successive lies, hypotheses, and dreams.

Emmanuel Levinas, captured by the Germans in 1940 and sent to a forest work detail with other Jewish prisoners of war, realized that in the eyes of his guards, and even of passersby, he and his fellow prisoners no longer belonged to the human race. Then a stray dog came and joined them: "For the dog, there was no doubt we were men."

A Reproachful Glance

In his poem "The Dog," Rainer Maria Rilke sums up the canine condition in four words: "Neither excluded nor included."

Rilke thought he saw Lou Andreas-Salomé's dog, just before it died, glance reproachfully at its mistress. And he promised himself never to run a similar risk. But he does recall the death of Salomé's dog in *The Notebooks of Malte Laurids Brigge,* as he is meditating on the fear of death: "For example, when my dog died." He declared to Maurice Betz:

> It may be that the dog sometimes finds a recompense for its endless adoration in the caresses of a suffering mistress, or in lying on the body of a dead master and licking his hand. Its eyes may then assume the almost human expression of the lion on the Unicorn Tapestry, and it has a brief glimpse of the burdensome existence it is led toward by humans, without pity or remorse.

In his short story "A Meeting," Rilke tells how a dog tries to get itself adopted by a stranger. The stranger refuses. It isn't out of cruelty or indifference. It's because he feels incapable of taking on such a responsibility.

> You wouldn't even notice how you were putting all your trust in me; you would overestimate me and expect of me what I'm not

capable of giving. You would observe me, and you would even approve of what isn't good. If I wanted to give you a special treat, could I produce one? And if one day you were sad and complained, would I be able to help you?—And you're really not supposed to think I'm the one who's letting you die.

In his preface for a book about cats, with drawings by the child who would one day become the painter Balthus, Rainer Maria Rilke declares that he regards the existence of felines as a shaky hypothesis at best. Dogs, on the other hand,

> approach us in such an admiring and trusting way that some of them seem to have abandoned their most primal canine traditions and have begun to worship our ways, even our faults. That is precisely what makes them tragic and sublime. Their determination to acknowledge us forces them to live at the very limits of their nature, constantly—through the humanness of their gaze, their nostalgic nuzzlings—on the verge of passing beyond those limits.

Rilke's most beautiful words on the subject are to be found in the *Notebooks of Malte Laurids Brigge*. Malte's mother tells how, several days after the young woman named Ingebord was buried, the dog Cavalier ran to greet her as if she had come back. He jumped all around and stood up on his hind legs as if to lick her face. Eventually he understood that he was making a fuss over something that wasn't there. So he lay down awkwardly on the ground and didn't move again.

In effect, Rilke reproaches animal life for not lasting as long as human life. Couldn't the same be said of love? With exceptions, love, like a dog, does not last as long as we do. A novel by Gertrude Stein, *Ida*, is almost entirely devoted to the enumeration of the heroine's dogs and husbands. In the same vein, Elizabeth von Arnim, a cousin of Katherine Mansfield and quite a cosmopolitan, wrote her autobiography via the story of her dogs: "though parents, husbands, children, lovers, and friends are all very well, they are not dogs."

Fourteen dogs succeeded one another in her heart. Each day, by the brevity of its life, our pet tells us, I shall soon be dead. In the deepest sense, these familiar creatures are part of the hurt of living. Because dogs inflict the suffering of loss upon us, the French sometimes call them "beasts of sorrow," *bêtes de chagrin*.

The World of Odors

"The only thing he can't do is talk," insist the good people who are amazed by their pet's intelligence. Octave Mirbeau feigns surprise that dogs can decode our language, at least when it refers to them: "They speak French, English, German, Russian, Greenlandic and Hindustani, Telugu, low Breton and low Norman, all the dialects and all the patois, without ever having learned them."

The French, perhaps even more than others, talk to their dogs and cats as if they were human. And they are totally surprised whenever their pet exhibits a sudden return to animality. When, for example, rediscovering its ancient instinct to camouflage itself for hunting, a dog rolls in shit. How could our favorite conversation partner—one whose wit, wisdom, and even (why not?) philosophy we so admire—go so far astray? Baudelaire takes up this theme in his prose poem "The Dog and the Flask." The creature described as the unworthy companion of Baudelaire's sorry existence resembles the reading public. Exasperated by delicate perfumes, it sniffs with delight at carefully selected garbage.

Henri Michaux, in *Passages*, remarks that you never see a dog stopping to smell a rose or a violet. Dogs are the cognescenti of foul odors.

They carry a goddamn dossier around in their heads, constantly updated. Who understands the menu of stink better? . . . They think about it. Got it! Now they know. These innocents come back to our sides without skipping a beat, full of affection and radiating a clear conscience.

Chesterton, in *The Flying Inn,* portrays the dog Quoddle as pitying humans for having so little sense of smell, a real handicap:

> They haven't got no noses
> They haven't got no noses
> And goodness only knowses
> The noselessness of Man!

Virginia Woolf's dog Flush would agree. The greatest poet knows only the rose and the dung heap, whereas the humblest dog lives in a world of smells. All it takes is one odor to unleash a million memories. "To him religion itself was smell." Virginia Woolf insists that neither Swinburne nor even Shakespeare would be capable of describing the infinity of odors perceived by Flush or of saying what they signify for him. But I will speak elsewhere and at greater length about Flush. He deserves it.

The psychoanalyst François Gantheret reminds us of the surprising capacities of certain hunting dogs, that will track game for miles and then, should they lose the scent, return on their own tracks, those tiny molecules of odor. This behavior is known as "hunting counter." The psychoanalyst sighs: "Ah! if only I were capable of returning on my own tracks as easily." But thought is slow, heavy, susceptible to the censure of repression. All we get are fragments, and with those it is difficult, not to say impossible, to recover the threads of our history.

Low Life

I've never been able to do without Baudelaire. Here again, I notice his fondness for lowlife dogs:

> I invoke the friendly, lively muse of cities to help me sing the song of the faithful dog, the mangy dog, the pitiful dog, the dog everybody kicks around because he is dirty and covered with fleas.

And a little farther on he repeats,

> I sing the mangy dog, the pitiful, the homeless dog, the roving dog, the circus dog. . . . I sing the luckless dog who wanders alone through the winding ravines of huge cities, or the one who blinks up at some poor outcast of society with its soulful eyes, as much as to say, "take me with you, and out of our joint misery we will make a kind of happiness."

This reminds me of the "Serenade for Hard Times," a hit from before World War II by the popular singer Perchicot. The hero of this song sees everyone as an ingrate except for a dog. This pooch, well cared for by rich owners, is the only one to recognize his former companion in misery:

> No matter times they ain't the best
> You come to me

Come, I still got my little nest
beneath the sky we'll be
A crust, a chop, the rest
It's yours for free.

Another little song, written by Scott Fitzgerald and Edmund Wilson during the Jazz Age, was one Fitzgerald liked to sing at parties:

Larger than a rat!
More faithful than a cat!
Dog! Dog! Dog!

Later, Scott Fitzgerald would write "Shaggy's Morning," the short story with a dog as its hero.

"Serenade for Hard Times" recaps the theme of Chaplin's masterpiece, *A Dog's Life.* Louis Delluc, the first film critic in France, believed that those three reels filmed in 1918 at the new First National Studios marked an era. "This tale, this film, this *pièta,* is the first complete work of art for cinema. This is a classic." (Delluc hadn't yet seen Griffith's films.) Charlie the tramp and Scraps the little white mutt with a black spot on one eye that gives him a scruffy look enjoy parallel destinies: misery, hunger, street scuffles, fear of the cops. All there is for shelter is a vacant lot with its wooden fence. Their condition improves only when man and dog get together. Thick as thieves, they manage to steal sausage and cakes from a roadside food stand.

The parallelism is largely created by two juxtaposed scenes: the one in the employment office where the tramp keeps losing his turn in line, and the scene where dogs fight Scraps for the morsel of food he has found in the street. There is yet another twist. As always in Chaplin's films, the charming Edna Purviance appears. As Charlie comes to Scraps's rescue during the dogfight, so he comes to Edna's rescue in a dance hall.

In short: a dog who leads a dog's life makes friends with two humans, a tramp and a dancer, who also lead a dog's life.

More than once in his ingenious mime scenes, Chaplin starts acting like a dog. In a film from the Keystone period, when caught chewing on his neighbor's lamb bone, he starts to growl and bark as though to say: "Excuse me. In a moment of aberration, I mistook myself for a dog." In another film, beaten up by the gigantic Eric Campbell, he lies down on the ground in that well-known submissive attitude of a dog admitting defeat.

The ending of *A Dog's Life*—a happy ending—has always left me perplexed. Charlie and Edna live out their love affair in the country, in a fairy-tale farmhouse. Scraps is there, gazing with pride at a litter of puppies. So Scraps is supposed to be a female?

Dogs' Paradise

Baudelaire imagined a special paradise for dogs: "Swedenborg confirms that there was one for the Turks and the Dutch!"

The dogs' paradise reminds me of a very old story.

Every night, coming home from work, my dog and I crossed the boulevard Saint-Germain. Often, a gentleman sitting at an outside table of a café, or just arriving there for his evening drink, would stop us and ask my permission to pet the dog, which I cheerfully granted. Ulysses could never get enough of being admired and coddled, as if he were perpetually lacking in affection. Among human traits this dog had appropriated, the primary one was narcissism.

The gentleman—tall, portly, around seventy—spoke with what I thought a Teutonic accent, so I decided that he was German.

While he was stroking my dog's coat, I couldn't help but notice his gold ring, set with a large diamond, a truly large one. At the end of these petting sessions the German always asked me:

"Would you allow me to give him a little chocolate?"

Although I explained that Ulysses didn't like chocolate, he insisted, and finally produced a piece from his pocket. He offered it to his friend, who took it to be polite, but spat it out immediately. I said, "You see."

This did not prevent the German from starting over again at the next meeting. Petting and chocolates.

Instead of proposing a delicacy that the dog didn't like, he would have done better to offer him his diamond. Or else the old man should have put Ulysses in his will and made him the beneficiary of the ring. This bad joke came into my head every time Ulysses spat out the chocolate.

When Ulysses died before his time, I was hoping to run into the German so that I could let him know. But the café where he used to sit was closed for remodeling and remained closed for a long time. After it reopened, the German never came back. Maybe he didn't like the new décor. It's red and mauve, frankly hideous.

Two years later, we crossed paths on the rue du Four. He was walking rather stiffly, jerkily, leaning on a rubber-tipped cane. I didn't fully recognize him until I saw him bending painfully over a dog that had come his way. I went up to him. Sure enough it was he, with the same diamond on his finger, the same German accent. But he was greatly changed. Probably a stroke. I saw he didn't recognize me.

"You used to give chocolate to my dog, a large Saint-Germain pointer."

"Yes, I love dogs."

I was disappointed. He loved all dogs, and I had thought he was interested specifically in mine. Still, as he left me, he added,

"Now he's in paradise with Saint Francis of Assisi."

A Dog with a Past

I have just been reminiscing about Ulysses. But I don't want to neglect Dick, a German braque–pointer mix, the inseparable companion of my childhood and adolescence.

In Pau, my father went to the café every night to play pinochle. He came home late, too late for us to wait up for him. One night, he came home with a dog called Dick. He explained that one of his friends had settled an old debt with him. I think he had lent him fifty francs. I don't know how much that is in today's money. And this strange friend had finally told him: "I'll never be in a position to pay you back, so take my dog."

Perhaps there are men who would give away their wife or their children like that, by way of repayment.

My father and his winnings were not well received. But Dick was such a friendly dog that we quickly adopted him. He belonged more to me than to the other members of the family. I walked him, and he followed me everywhere. He was on the lookout for me when I was due home from high school. But he had only to see a shotgun and he forgot who I was. His hunting past took over. The rest of the time he feared my father, fled him, and took refuge between my legs when my father tried to give him orders.

Happily, my father was more of a fisherman than a hunter. When we had spent the day in Saint-Engrâce, deep in the

Basque country, dying of boredom while my father tried to catch trout, and were driving home at night in an old open-top Citroën, my little sister and I had Dick as our living blanket in the back seat. He stretched out on our knees. He kept us warm.

Hunting was not the only thing that separated us. Dick was a wanderer. He went off on his own for long escapades throughout the city. I discovered that he was making the rounds of bistros, looking for his former master. If I happened into one of the large cafés in his company, he would make a fuss over the cashier. He knew every cashier in every café in the city of Pau.

Dick followed me everywhere except to school. I remember the little fox terrier Rita, our dog in Caen, who was still alive when we moved to Pau and burst into the classroom one day while the pious and devoted Mademoiselle Marie was teaching us to read. I was severely scolded, though my only fault was that Rita loved me. I was five or six years old at the time. Later, when I was in high school, Dick bounded down the boulevard des Pyrénées and knocked one of my teachers down—which did not contribute to my own good standing. Between the two of us we were frequently in trouble. We got lost in a storm in the mountains of the Basque country, and when we finally came home, soaking wet, Dick got yelled at as much as I did. At St. Martin's Fair, held every November, we weren't satisfied to watch the black-suited Pierrot presiding over his lottery, so one year we went for a ride on the Big Eight.* How could they have allowed us to get into the little car? Dick, who quickly panicked, tried to jump out, and I clung to his collar to hold him back. We nearly went over-

*Roger Grenier's *Another November* (published in translation by the University of Nebraska Press, 1998) tells of a Pierrot, the lovestruck figure of the commedia dell'arte, who presided each year over a lottery game at St. Martin's Fair in Pau but was always dressed in black silk instead of the traditional white.

board. Those were the follies of our youth. Not nearly as bad as adult follies.

The rest of the time, Dick liked to lie on an overstuffed armchair near the window, his muzzle on the arm rest, pensive, dreaming perhaps of sawdust and cigarette butts under marble café tables.

Flaubert, from Python to Parrot

Sartre spoke about the anguish of dogs in the context of Flaubert. According to Sartre, it drove Gustave crazy in his childhood, as it does dogs, when he understood that he didn't understand. I would add that Flaubert, once he became a writer, could describe better than anyone the complexity of the exchanges and the immensity of the love between a human and an animal. But he didn't take dogs as an example. No doubt he needed more exotic animals. He imagined Salammbô copulating with his python. But let us not forget Flaubert's simple-hearted Félicité and her parrot Loulou, which, even after being stuffed, remains alive for Félicité and guides her to the gates of heaven the day she dies.

A Simple Heart, built around a deliberately pitiful anecdote, takes in at a glance a huge field that few writers have explored in a satisfactory manner. Félicité's love for the parrot Loulou is at once a defense against tremendous solitude, a substitute for her nephew who died in a distant and exotic land, a game, and a secret celebration. Flaubert himself says it best: "In her isolation Loulou was almost like a son, a lover to her. He would climb up to her fingers, nibble her lips, cling to her bodice."

A pet is a protection against life's insults, a defense against the world, the somewhat vain conviction of being truly loved, a way of being both less alone and more alone.

The Walk down the Rue du Bac

For years I used to walk Ulysses in our neighborhood, so we ended up knowing a lot of people. Dogs are like Emmanuel Kant, who always wanted to take the same walk. The less it changes, the happier they are. Leaving the house, we would turn left. Unless, inadvertently, I uttered the word "Tuileries," in which case there was nothing to be done; Ulysses would turn right and I had to follow him. We would march across the rue de Varenne under the surveillance of the policemen who guard the intersection in front of Matignon, the official residence of the prime minister. These security police, many of them from rural areas, would compliment the Saint-Germain pointer on his beauty or ask me about his hunting skills. Depending on the day, I would lie or tell the truth, the truth being that he didn't hunt.

A little farther on, Dora, the big black dog that guarded the Catholic Rescue Mission, would have smelled our arrival. She would start to cry with emotion, with desire. She would thrust her muzzle through the bars of the gate to kiss her beloved. Dora, the black sinner in a pious community of bishops, priests, saintly women.

The next house belonged to the writer Romain Gary. On our first outing at 7:30 in the morning, we would often meet him strolling down the street, going to buy the newspaper or to have a cup of coffee across the way. Gary said that the rue du Bac was his country. Tartar, Jew, Russian, Pole: he was a mix of so many things that he had no desire to be a citizen of the world, a European, or even a Frenchman. What he required was membership in a tiny province or someplace even smaller. Hence the rue du Bac. "Come here, you jerk," he would say to Ulysses, who would advance immediately, stretch his hind legs, and rub up against him.

One day in September 1980, we met Gary near the front of his building. As usual, he said, "Come here, you jerk!" We approached. I said to Romain: "I'm afraid this is the last time you'll see Ulysses. He's going to be put to sleep."

Romain let out a violent sob and hid in his entryway.

Ulysses died September 23; Gary died December 2.

In one year, Gary's former wife (the actress Jean Seberg), Gary himself, and Ulysses all died, and the street was empty. I might as well speak of all three in the same breath, since we loved one another.

We would pass the Clermont-Tonnerre mansion, where Chateaubriand spent the last ten years of his life. From there, we'd follow the same short path the writer used to take to Madame Récamier's house at the Abbaye-aux-Bois, a stone's throw from Sèvres-Babylone. But in the end, he was paralyzed and she was blind.

The concierge of one of the most aristocratic abodes on our street always had small dogs, which gave us a chance to stop for a moment and exchange dog talk. On one encounter she announced the death of a little fox terrier, more than fourteen years old, and added, "Since Easter is coming and we're going home to the country, my daughter has put her in the fridge."

Walking the length of the Bon Marché department store, we'd take the rue Babylone down to Boucicaut Square. Our car was parked there, in the underground garage. Ulysses would push his luck and take to the stairs. No, not today, no car, no walk in the "dog meadow" at the Bois de Boulogne. Just a turn around this wretched square, made even uglier by a block of lard purporting to represent that do-gooder Madame Boucicaut, surrounded by charitable ladies. The turn around the square was always counterclockwise. Sometimes during our last nightly outing I would cross paths with shadows that already belonged to the past: the Italian filmmaker Marcello Pagliero, the male lead in *Rome Open City*, walking a little dog; the singer Marianne Oswald, who ended her days in a rented room on the attic floor of the Hotel Lutétia (Marianne once appeared dressed as a red flame reciting Cocteau's *Anna la bonne*); an old gentleman on roller skates, dragged down the street by two labradors and guaranteed to fall flat on his face. In the square, a strange bag lady dressed in khaki, a French flag and the word "patriot" sewn on her knapsack, had set up on a bench for the night. Her bicycle was beside her. She said she was General de Gaulle's niece. One day she too disappeared. The city creates phantoms, then swallows them up.

Once in awhile this bag lady would come to Gallimard, the publishing house where I work, claiming that her manuscript had been stolen. On one occasion she asked to see Gaston Gallimard. "But Monsieur Gallimard is dead," the receptionist said, only too happy to have an irrefutable alibi at her disposal. "That's not true," the bag lady replied. "I saw him at Jean-Paul Sartre's funeral." (Sartre was still alive.)

Once we'd finished our tour of the square, it was time to start for home.

At night, too, I used to spot Roland Dubillard, who lived in the same building as Gary, crossing the street to buy a bottle of whiskey at Pulcinella's, a grocery that stayed open late. I mention Dubillard because he, like Rilke, refused to love dogs for fear of making them suffer: "It would hurt me to make a dog suffer, a dog that was mine by virtue of that suffering and of everything that made that suffering possible. That's why I hate dogs."

Many years earlier, when I was working as a journalist,

Nicole Ladmiral, the star of Robert Bresson's film, *Diary of a Country Priest,* had asked me to interview Dubillard, who wasn't as well known as he deserved to be. We sat a good half hour face-to-face without speaking. My method was to say nothing, because people usually can't tolerate silence. So they start to confess. But with him it didn't work. In the end we burst out laughing. This good memory is associated with a tragic one: the awful death of Nicole Ladmiral, who threw herself under a Metro train.

I'm quite glad to have Chateaubriand for a neighbor. His amorous adventures amuse me. But it was still more exciting, during World War II, to walk down the rue d'Amsterdam every day on my way to work and to pass the Hôtel de Dieppe, where Baudelaire lived. Or, even today (to stay close to the rue du Bac), I'm happy when I cross the rue Paul-Louis Courier, formerly called the Passage Sainte-Marie, and remember Stendhal: "Suddenly I see myself in a room on the third floor, with a view of the rue du Bac; you entered this lodging from the Passage Sainte-Marie, so beautiful and so changed today. A humble staircase led to my garret room."

He insists that he was very ill there and almost died. But he had already convinced himself that the ultimate happiness was to live in a garret in Paris and to write. On the same corner where the young Henri Beyle had his room in 1799, there now sits a café. With the first ray of sun, a crowd mobs the outside tables, while the boulevard Saint-Germain stretches out below like an arm of the sea. This is our beach.

Our village has always attracted writers. I can identify my neighbors in the portraits adorning the windows of the Gallimard bookshop on the boulevard Raspail. Most of them are alive, and I meet them on the street. But sometimes I see the faces of friends who have gone. The photo of Romain Gary that they have there adds to my sadness because it shows Gary holding his dog Pancho in his arms, a dog that looks at you seriously, almost severely, and that died in Majorca, run over by a car. When that portrait is on display, a visit to the bookshop feels like a pilgrimage.

On June 19, 1841, more than forty years after starting out on the rue du Bac, Stendhal wrote to Romain Colomb from Citavecchia: "I have two dogs, which I love tenderly. One is a black English spaniel, a handsome dog, but sad and melancholic. The other, Lupetto, is café au lait, gay, lively—a young Burgundian, in short. It made me sad to have nothing to love."

Four months later, Stendhal left Citavecchia forever. Nine months later he was dead. What became of his dogs?

When you love a dog and it loves you, the lack of synchronization between human and animal life is bound to bring sorrow. I remember a phone call from Madame Simone: "My dog has died. You seem to know about these things. Could you tell me where I might get another?"

She was 95 at the time. What optimism! Perhaps she was right, since she lived to be 107, some say 110. So she still had just about the duration of a canine existence before her.

To Be Loved

People with dogs, writes Colette Audry in *Behind the Bathtub*, have "discovered a haven even safer and more private than their mother's bosom."

There is masochism in a love like this, and other times sadism, the possibility of keeping a helpless being in one's power. Animals' executioners know that their victim will always love them. Like the old man Salamano in Camus's *The Stranger*. For eight years, Salamano insulted and beat his dog, but they made an inseparable couple and even ended up looking alike. Besides, the old man had given himself the dog as a present after his wife died, to replace her. In *The Fall*, Clamence says he likes dogs "because they always forgive." One exception is Kafka's dog Karo, who hates his master, the hunter, although "this dubious person is not in the least worthy of it." Another is Kafka's allegorical tale, "Jackals and Arabs," where the jackals are like dogs in the negative. "They are our dogs, finer dogs than yours," an Arab says. But he adds—and with this the tale ends—"And how they hate us!"

(Kafka's story brings back a memory. In 1941, when I was a soldier in Constantine, we took a jackal into our unit—though I don't remember how it happened. He was an affectionate little beast and jumped from bed to bed during nap time, looking to be petted. No different from a dog. Unfortunately he was covered with lice, and since we were in the middle of a typhus epidemic, we couldn't keep him.)

Perhaps those who love their dogs the most are, by that very fact, executioners. Here Sartre isn't wrong: too close a proximity to humans makes domestic animals unhappy. They spend their time observing their master, figuring out what he's going to do with them. Everything is a sign: a cough, a glance at a watch, turning off the television. There is no innocent act. Every minute carries its ration of anguish.

A dog, yes, but . . .

If we get a dog, is it for the dog's happiness or, quite selfishly, for our own? Kafka's "Blumenfeld, an Elderly Bachelor" verges on caricature—and of course one can sense here Kafka's persistent need for self-accusation—in its portrait of a solitary man tempted to get himself a companion. The bachelor is like a spinster who dreams of having an inferior creature near her—a cat, a canary, if not a few goldfish. She would even be happy with a house plant. What Blumenfeld likes about dogs is that they are amusing, appreciative, faithful. But he soon comes up with objections. A dog is filthy and the bachelor is maniacally clean. A dog carries fleas. A dog can fall ill and you don't know how to treat it, nor whether the illness is temporary or serious and contagious. Whatever it is, it's repugnant.

But the worst is yet to come. One day you find you've grown old. You haven't had the courage to get rid of your dog in time, "and then comes the moment when your own age peers out at you from the dog's oozing eyes. You have to cope with the half-blind, weak-lunged animal all but immobile with fat, and in this way pay dearly for the pleasures the dog once had given."

Hence, no dog. The selfish bachelor is sorry. The ideal, for him, would be an animal that required almost no care, that he could kick from time to time and send out to sleep on the street on the condition that it would be ready to lick his hand and bark a welcome any time he wanted it to.

A nasty, unfinished tale, probably intended to show Felice Bauer that its author was unfit to marry.

Friends of Animals

Paul Léautaud provides us with a caricature of a friend of animals. He was famous for his love of cats. I once heard him demand that the miners on strike in northern France be shot.

After all, Hitler loved his dogs. To the point of dragging his favorite, Blondi, and her litter with him to his death! And in the same class as Léautaud, or even better than he, was Axel Munthe, an author who once enjoyed a fair reputation. Malaparte visited Munthe in his retreat in Capri and talked to him about the Germans who were massacring Jews, workers, and peasants, setting cities and villages on fire. Axel Munthe got worried and asked if it was true that they were killing birds. Malaparte replied that they didn't have time. They were too busy exterminating humans.

"At least the Germans are not killing birds," said Axel Munthe with a smile. "I am very glad they are not killing birds."

Malaparte, who never flinched at a contradiction, would later applaud the political reeducation camps in China, although he was indignant because no dogs could be seen in the streets and the Chinese were barbaric enough to force-feed their geese.

Our Great Men

I suppose we should include Napoleon in our survey of men of letters who have spoken of dogs. In the *Memorial of Saint Helena,* he tells how he was once walking on a battlefield in Italy from which the dead had not yet been removed. He saw a dog beside the body of its master, howling, licking the dead man's face. "No incident, on any of my battlefields, ever produced so deep an impression on me" ("my battlefields"—what a remarkable possessive!), declares Napoleon, who insisted elsewhere that the deaths of a million meant nothing to him. "I had, without emotion, ordered battles which were to decide the fate of the army; I had beheld, with a dry eye, the execution of those operations, by which numbers of my countrymen were sacrificed; and here I was upset, my feelings roused, by the mournful howling of a dog."

When Josephine married Bonaparte, she refused to kick a pug named Fortuné out of her bed. Fortuné was used to sleeping with her, so the general was forced to share the Creole beauty's bed with her dog.

Historians have much to teach us about the dogs of the great men who have held sway over our poor world. Henri Maspero managed to find the names of Ashurbanipal's dogs. Some scholars have even researched the lives of animals that became, in a sense, historical figures in their own right. Thus the fox terrier on His Master's Voice records has emerged from anonymity. His name turns out to have been Nipper (1884–95). His master was the English painter Francis Barraud (1856–1924), who sold his dog's portrait to the Gramophone Company for the sum of one hundred pounds.

Apollinaire, in the snippets he contributed to the *Mercure de France* in 1917 and 1918, which are—let's face it—nothing but platitudes, cites dogs that were made kings. He recycles stories that have come down to us through Elianos and Pliny. He tells about Suening, a dog proclaimed king of Norway by a prince seeking vengeance around AD 230. What contempt one must have for dogs, to want to make kings of them!

Indeed, a king of Bavaria, Othon, acted like a dog and ate dog food from a bowl on the ground, without using his hands.

Looking at the chronicles, letters, poems, and paintings from the Middle Ages on, it is amazing to see the number of dogs with which kings and noblemen surrounded themselves.

The fierce Agrippa d'Aubigné, dissatisfied with the peace treaty negotiated at Bergerac, wrote an exceptionally violent farewell letter to Henri de Navarre. Around the same time, in Agen, he encountered a large spaniel named Citron that had previously slept in the king's bed. The abandoned dog appeared to be starving. D'Aubigné sent it to board with a woman and had a vengeful poem sewn to the fur on the dog's neck:

> The faithful Citron who lay before
> On your sacred bed, now lies on hard ground
> (. . .) And therefore does endure
> Hunger, cold, beatings, disdain and insult
> Customary payment for service to kings.

The next day, Henri de Navarre passed through Agen. The townspeople used the occasion to bring the dog before him. Reading the poem, Henri blanched.

D'Aubigné was not yet twenty-seven years old. There would be time for him to reconcile with the ungrateful Henri IV.

Clément Marot, a poet who drew his inspiration from a more delicate source, describes Eleanor of Hapsburg, the wife of Francis I, taking her little dog Mignonne into her bed every night:

> So sleeps the little frisky one
> Atop the alabaster breasts.
>
> What cleanliness! How delicate!
>
> And if she wants to go and piss,
> Neither sheets nor spread shall she soil
> But her mistress scratch, scratch
> With her delicate paw,
> Warning her to take her down,
> To wipe her off.

Here I suspect that Marot is copying Martial's celebration of Issa, Publius's little dog: "If she needs something, don't worry about her soiling the bedclothes; for she warns with a movement of her paw that she has to be taken down from the bed, and asks next to be wiped off."

Unlike Marot, who paints an indulgent portrait of Queen Eleanor in bed with Mignonne, Saint-Simon takes the Duke of Vendôme to task. The duke, it must be said, pushed cohabitation with the canine species quite a bit farther: "His filth was extreme, and he bragged about it. Fools thought he was a simple man. His bed was always full of dogs and bitches that littered by his side. As for his own habits in that bed, he never held anything in."

It was a strange sort of love that Charles IX felt for his dog Courte. When she died, he had gloves made from her skin. And Ronsard wasn't afraid to use her as an example of devotion to the royal person.

At the age of five, the future Louis XIII gave bread to a dog and was reprimanded by a lady at court.

"Monsieur, one should not give bread to dogs. One should give it to the poor."

The child replied: "Are dogs rich?"

Louis XIV, forgetting his majesty for once, portrayed himself in some lines whose double meaning should not be discounted:

> With his ministers he might well confer
> But as soon as he sees his bitch
> He leaves them all for her;
> Nothing can stop him when the hunt calls.

Did little Louis XVII have a dog with him at the Prison du Temple or not? Witnesses later claimed that the child had always been afraid of dogs. But his jailer's widow said he had a pet dog in prison named Coco. So either she was lying, or the child was not really Louis XVII, since Louis XVII hated dogs.

Next we come to a paradox. Whether in Europe or in America, politicians who arrange to be seen with a pet by their side are attempting to show that they have a heart. A 1944 campaign speech by Roosevelt has gone down in history as the Fala speech because the president, in an effort to captivate his audience, spoke at length about his Scottish terrier Fala. To appear human, French politicians too like to be seen with a labrador, a pointer, or a setter, especially if there are cameras around. André Malraux, in *Felled Oaks: Conversations with De Gaulle*, doesn't go so far as to have the general escorted by a dog. But he does improve the austere décor of the great man's residence by having a silent companion on the premises, observing him when he plays solitaire and following him on his walks: "A big gray chartreux jumps onto the desk. Where does he come from?"

Yes, where does he come from? For it seems that General de

Gaulle never had a cat. But Malraux put cats everywhere and even made the silhouette of a tomcat part of his signature.

Baltique, a black labrador that comforted François Mitterrand in his final days, made a spectacular appearance at her master's funeral, demonstrating remarkable dignity. Eventually she was adopted by one of the president's bodyguards, who was accustomed to walking her. And that was certainly the best solution for her.

In one of his couplets, the poet Paul-Jean Toulet puts great men in their place:

My dog was named Tom, and my bitch Djaly,
Ah, how many pompous names are more deserving of obscurity.

Heroes and Refugees

Casimir Delavigne celebrates a dog that was wounded on the barricades during the 1830 revolution.

The First World War, that great devourer of heroes or, more accurately, victims, did not fail to enlist the canine nation. Paul Morand, in an August 1916 entry to his *Diary of an Embassy Attaché*, cites a special attraction on the program at the Nice casino: "The dog that has received the Medal of Honor, presented by its master, Sergeant P."

In 1940, animals escaped promotions and decorations alike. Georges Duhamel alone holds the distinction of passionately celebrating canine behavior in June 1940, when France fell to the Germans. He evokes these memories of the exodus from Paris in an article in *Le Figaro:*

> I am going to say what I know, what I think, and what I have understood about the suffering of dogs during this collapse of our world. . . . On a number of occasions I even had the feeling that these refugee dogs understood the magnitude of the event and the immensity of our misfortune better than we humans did.

Which earned Georges Duhamel the privilege of being skewered by Camus in a satiric piece in *Combat* signed with the pseudonym Suetonius and entitled: "Fido and the Defeat."

This is nothing compared to the story of Bobby, a Skye terrier owned by René Lefèvre, star of the *Crime of Monsieur Lange*—as related by Dr. Merry, a society vet who never tired of telling stories that are a little too good to be true. During the Occupation, René Lefèvre lived in a property above the Cap d'Antibes. Every day a German soldier would pass the front gate, carrying the ration of soup for his company. Bobby was attracted by the smell. His master reprimanded him, and the dog lost interest in the parade of mess tins with their good meaty odor. Bobby was not going to be a collaborator. Then René Lefèvre was denounced and had to leave and go into hiding. The dog remained alone on the property. Having developed a hatred for the enemy all on his own, Bobby growled and barked, his mouth foaming, every time he saw a soldier walking by. The epilogue is tragic: before they packed up their bags, the German soldiers pillaged the villa and strangled Bobby, the resistance dog.

Larbaud, or Bourgeois Follies

The triumphant bourgeoisie drafts animals not only for its wars but for its other follies as well. On Valery Larbaud's country estate at Valbois in the Bourbonnais region of central France, a long, majestic, tree-lined walkway leads to a wood that drops sharply into a narrow ravine. In this little wood the Larbauds had constructed a double stone stairway leading to a large rock that they called "the Tomb of Brutus" because, Larbaud claimed, a family dog by that name was buried there.

In January 1932, Larbaud traveled to Milan, accompanied by his dog Barty. It amused him to observe which people liked dogs and which didn't. A lady asked if she might pet Barty. A taxi driver wanted to know how much he cost. High marks for the people of Milan. But a customs agent asked him if the dog barked in German. "In Scots," responded Larbaud. Barty was a Scottish terrier.

A month later the dog and his master were in Rome. At that time, the fascists had installed a real wolf and a real eagle at the top of the Capitoline Hill. Larbaud took Barty to see these living symbols. "He seemed duly impressed, and so did the she-wolf," he noted in his diary. And he felt the need to write about it to his friend Marcel Ray: "I showed the she-wolf to Barty and Barty to the she-wolf; she jumped up and down in her cage while he watched her with surprise and a little *paura*."

The next day, in another letter: "Barty must be in love with the she-wolf. When we tell him "la lupa!" he runs to the window and watches for her."

As Samuel Butler put it (and he happens to have been translated into French by the very same Valery Larbaud): "The great pleasure of a dog is that you may make a fool of yourself with him and not only will he not scold you, but he will make a fool of himself, too."

Identification

Dog and owner wind up thinking of each other as more or less a part of themselves.

One night, on the Champ de Mars, Ulysses disappeared. I finally located him in the darkness of a side street. He had just made love to a female Dalmatian. The two lovers were still locked together. The Dalmatian's mistress, an elegant foreigner—the kind of woman you see at embassies—put her dog back on the leash. She was very irritated. For ten minutes—ten minutes, the time it took for the couple to detach, is a long time—she uttered not a word to me. As if I were the guilty party, as if it were I who had assailed the virtue of the dog or even, perhaps, of the lady.

Another night, on the rue du Bac, Ulysses stopped in the middle of the street to attend to his needs, close to a building of a distinctive architecture that Joseph Losey used as the location for his film *Monsieur Klein.* An archway extends into an alley, and way in the back is a small private house, occupied at the time by an important statesman. It was probably a secret rendezvous for politicians. While the dog was thus occupied, a taxi stopped. The distinguished political analyst Raymond Aron alighted. I prayed he wouldn't see me, attached as I was to the end of a leash of an animal busy defecating. A prayer unanswered. He walked toward me, spoke to me, while Ulysses remained in his shameful position. Finally, Raymond Aron was engulfed by the archway, en route to his important secret meeting.

In the myth of Tristan and Iseult, two dogs play a role. In the interests of time, I'll forget about Pticru, the gift from a fairy, although much could be said about what he symbolizes. I'll concentrate instead on Hodain, Tristan's little pointer, a metaphor for fidelity. Hodain sheds tears when his master is far away. When Tristan brings Iseult to see the king on the eve of his departure, she asks him to soften the blow of their separation:

"Tristan, let me ask you something. Leave me Hodain, your dog. I think that when I see him, I shall often remember you. If my heart is sad, seeing him will bring me joy."

"Lady, you keep Hodain. I beg you, for the love of God, look after him. Just as you have loved me, love him."

At that moment, the dog is not only the image of fidelity. He becomes a substitute for the man. He is identified with Tristan, to the point where he too drinks the fatal love potion. In the thirteenth-century English version entitled *Sire Tristrem*, the dog licks the cup after the hero has finished drinking from it. "They were both obviously in love and happy. Together they would taste both the joy and the pain."

When Tristan returns home, disguised as a madman, it is the dog that recognizes him, not Iseult. In the crudest fashion, and in vain, Tristan reminds his lover of the time he carried her across the ford: "You slipped to the ground and you spread those pretty thighs for me, with everyone watching." She still doesn't want to recognize him. And then Tristan says: "He remembers the master who trained and raised him better than you remember the man who loved you so. There is great nobility in the dog and great disloyalty in woman." This misogynist theme is found frequently in the Middle Ages. But we have already seen it in the *Odyssey*.

In everyday life, we often notice that dogs and their owners end up looking alike, perhaps because people unconsciously choose an animal that resembles them. There are boxer men and Pekingese women. Don Quixote's dog, seen by Goya, is as thin as the sad-faced knight.

Goya! And then there is that enigmatic painting of his in the Prado, *Perro enterrado en arena* (Dog buried in the sand). It is a large, quasi-abstract canvas, a geometry of spots of varying degrees of darkness, with nothing but a dog's head at the bottom. Why is he buried in the sand? For fun? Highly unlikely. Probably for torture. The despair of dying in absolute solitude, without understanding, as he raises his eyes in vain toward an empty sky.

Vocation

Lacking divine protection, we ought to implore canine protection. Junichirō Tanizaki tells in the memoirs of his childhood how, as early as primary school, when the brush he used to draw characters was worn out, he would stick it between the paws of the stone dogs guarding the temple of Lord Tenjin. It was a local custom. Tenjin was believed to make you skilled in the art of writing. Stone dogs may have determined the vocation of one of Japan's greatest writers.

Fantasies, Symbols, Signals

Monsieur Du Boysaimé, a graduate of the École Polytechnique who participated in Bonaparte's expedition to Egypt, devised an equation for "the curve made by a dog running after its master." His memoirs, published in 1811, are referred to both by Lautréamont and by Jules Verne. Each writer writes within his means, using his favorite inspiration, and, if you'll forgive me the expression, each hangs his fantasies on his dog's tail.

In *Adive*, André Pieyre de Mandiargues portrays a woman waiting in the dark for another woman. Without understanding at first what is going on, she is visited by a bitch, who makes marvelous love to her. In Faulkner's short story "The Dog," a howling animal looks for its murdered master, with the blind obstinacy of fate.

Alina Reyes calls one of her books *The Dog That Wanted to Eat Me*. In her early childhood she was protected by a dog, and later, in the Pyrenees, a large sheepdog saved her life by sounding the alarm when her carriage ran off the road and almost fell into a ditch. She recalls another, very scary dog that she was afraid of meeting in the forest. But most important was the dog that appeared in her dreams, a ferocious creature, "the messenger of time." This German shepherd held a hand in its jaws. A hand that was also a sheet of paper. A premonition of the writer's destiny?

The dog can also serve as a symbol. Cervantes, for example, speaks of "alabaster casts on tombs of the people who lie buried within; when they are man and wife, they place between their feet the effigy of a dog, to signify that in life the friendship and fidelity they observed was inviolable."

What does that skinny dog signify at the foot of the statue of Rabbi Loew, the Maharal, in Prague? Alongside the dog is a nude young woman. There is surely a symbol here, but of what? What game is at play in the wisdom of the old man, the frail nudity of the young woman, and the perplexed look of the dog? Sylvie Germain describes this statue in *Bursts of Salt*, a novel set in Prague.

Agrippa d'Aubigné describes a "funereal black dog" that "barked" within the heart of Cardinal Crescentio during the Council of Trent. This dog, symbol of a demon, appears before the cardinal, announcing his impending death and damnation:

> It never left you since the day it made you see
> Your pain, the evil, death, despair, your destiny.

Goethe may not have been familiar with these lines by the Protestant poet, but he had read a seventeenth-century work, J. L. Gottfried's *Chronicles* (1619). An illustration from this book shows a big black dog that appears before Cardinal Crescentio. Goethe may have been thinking of this dog when he had Mephistopheles surge forth in the guise of a water spaniel.

We often associate dogs with death and attribute a supernatural prescience to them. A friend of Flaubert's, Alfred le Poittevin, died on Monday, April 3, 1848. And Flaubert wrote:

> On Wednesday I was out walking all afternoon with a dog that followed me without my having called her (this dog had grown fond of Alfred and always accompanied him when he was walking by himself. The night before his death she howled horribly, and no one could make her stop.)

Equally symbolic is the hound of the Baskervilles, harbinger of terror. Not to mention its offspring, which populate novels and horror films.

Sometimes a dog serves as a signal. The white Pomeranian in Chekhov's "Lady with Lapdog" is both a decorative object and a sign which, in the semantics of love, announces that the lady is alone, ready for adventure. Indeed, it is by virtue of that dog—a classic strategy—that Gourov makes his first move. "What good fellows dogs are!" said Chekhov.

In Pirandello, too, we encounter a lady with a little dog. But the situation is diabolical. Liri, Livia's pet, no longer knows whom he should devote himself to. He loves the lady's husband, but he also loves her two lovers. And the signs of his love lead to a fine mess.

These little dogs have a medieval precursor in *The Lady of Vergi*. In this famous rhymed tale from the thirteenth century, the amiable chatelaine, who only wishes to see her lover in secret, orders her *petit chienet,* her little doggy, to go alone to the orchard where her knight is hiding, thus signaling that the coast is clear.

Even more striking, in one of La Fontaine's tales, "The Little Dog," the fairy Manto transforms himself into a dog in order to encourage the guilty love affair between the beautiful Argie, wife of a judge, and the chivalrous young Atis.

Metaphysics

Repeatedly, and to this day, the dog furnishes our greatest thinkers with metaphors. Spinoza, in a much analyzed passage of the *Ethics* (proposition 17), reflects upon a simile used by Jewish and Islamic philosophers, including Philo, Maimonides, and Averroës:

> To say a word, too, here about the intellect and will which we commonly attribute to God—if intellect and will pertain to His eternal essence, these attributes cannot be understood in the sense in which men generally use them, for the intellect and will which could constitute His essence would have to differ entirely from our intellect and will, and could resemble ours in nothing except in name. There could be no further likeness than that between the celestial constellation of the Dog and the animal which barks.

My friend the photographer Brassaï, whom I was more accustomed to seeing in his study, holding forth on Goethe, Nietzsche, and Proust, than with a camera around his neck, wrote the following on the title page of a book about Hermann Lotze's metaphysics:

We run around the present as a dog, being walked, runs around its master. Sometimes it is in front, sometimes behind, happy to sniff at its master's footsteps. It is never really with him except on the rare occasion when it takes the lump of sugar that's offered.

Voltaire versus Rousseau

To be known as a friend of animals isn't always a good thing. Remember the accident that befell Jean-Jacques Rousseau as he was coming down from Ménilmontant on October 24, 1776. He was knocked over by a Great Dane, which ran in front of Monsieur de Saint-Fargeau's carriage. He suffered a serious concussion, and a rumor circulated in Paris that he had died. Voltaire, rather nastily under the circumstances, wrote to the writer Florian (did he hope his correspondent would make one of his fables out of it?):

> Jean-Jacques did well to die. They claim it isn't true that it was a dog that killed him; he recovered from the wounds inflicted by his comrade the dog; but they say that on December 12 he got it into his head to celebrate the Escalade [a Swiss holiday] in Paris with an old citizen of Geneva named Romilly; he ate like a devil and, having given himself indigestion, died like a dog.

Jean-Jacques did have a dog, which he called Duc. Then, out of fear of displeasing his noble protectors—which wasn't like him—he decided against the name Duc and renamed his dog Turc. To his great embarrassment, he had to explain this change of names before an assembly including two or three dukes: "What was offensive about the name *Duc* in this story was not so much that I had given it to my dog as that I had taken it away from him."

Nearly the same thing happened to me. I wanted to call my dog Ubu, because it was the year of U's.* Emmanuel Peillet, alias Sainmont, alias Latis, alias Mélanie le Plumet, soul of the parodic association known as the College of Pataphysics (founded in memory of Alfred Jarry, the author of *Ubu Roi*) forbade it. He was simply upholding the *utmost* standard of derision on behalf of the pataphysicians:

> It would not be very respectful to call your dog Ubu (not respectful, I mean for Our Father). It would be banal to call him Ulysses (I've known some). But you're left with: Utile, Ulfilas, Ulric, Unique, Uranus, if you're not afraid that will lead him to homosexuality (you can make it French by saying Urane, as they did in the seventeenth century), Ursus, Uriel, Ugolin, Uléma, Uhu, Ut [French for the musical note C] (you could train him to come to that note on the piano, the oboe, the saxophone, etc.). Ultimate isn't bad either. If you're not repelled by Latin, you have Uber (fertile), Ultor (vengeful). Greek? You have Utope (as in Utopia, he is nowhere), Usmim (combative), Ure (tail; it is a French word in the *dasyure* composites, etc.), Ulē (matter, if you are a Cartesian, it's written also Rylē), Upsi (up high! so he can pose). The Hebrew Ul (body), Uhel (proper name of a man). You will tell me that is pronounced "oo": OK, but it's transcribed with a *u*—for example, Uriah (Bathsheba's husband, cuckolded by David). I forgot Urbane (if he's polite), and certainly there are others.

I called my dog Ulysses.

---

*The French tend to observe the convention of giving purebred dogs names that begin with the official letter for the year of their birth; the letters change according to the alphabet, allowing you to tell how old a dog is from its name.—Trans.

First Prize

In books, people treat animals as they treat them in life. With greater or lesser sincerity, intelligence, love, disdain, indifference. In putting together a little literary anthology, one inevitably finds oneself running a contest, passing out high or low grades. I would be happy to give a zero to Borges, who made no distinction among dogs, mixing up all the breeds into one. Many writers are too narcissistic ever to burden themselves with an animal. Liking neither dogs nor cats, they only know them secondhand, as it were.

Jacques Brenner, who, like St. Roch, is always and everywhere accompanied by a dog, edited a radical *Plea on Behalf of Dogs* as part of a series of books titled "Idée Fixe." Brenner, who in a number of his books has proved a good historian of literature, reviews his literary judgments here in the light of a single criterion: attitude toward the animal kingdom. The number one enemy is Descartes, of course, because of his theory of animal-machines. And since the philosopher believed our souls to be immortal, Brenner thinks he is alive today, reincarnated as a performing dog in some circus—which immediately makes him likable.

Brenner praises the author of the *Marriage of Figaro,* who had his dog's collar engraved with the words, "My name is Mademoiselle Follette. Monsieur de Beaumarchais belongs to me." And Lamartine is also approved of, not because he sang of Elvire but because his wife complained, "He only loves his dogs."

Gide gets a place of honor: "To justify his morals, he referred not to Plato, Shakespeare, or Michaelangelo but rather to dogs and ducks." Giono too does well: he wrote that the moral responsibility of murder is of the same order whether one kills a man or an animal. Bernard Shaw, a vegetarian, is a prince of the soul. Marguerite Yourcenar deserves a high grade. I wouldn't deny it. When she signed my copy of her book *A Coin in Nine Hands,* she confessed, "Yesterday all I thought about was your beautiful dog."

Brenner has mixed feelings about the poet Francis Jammes. He sang touchingly of donkeys and calves. But he was too attached to the hunt. Let's not even talk about Mauriac. Two months before he died, he wrote that if he could begin his life again, he could imagine living on a property from which dogs and cats were banished. But he would be glad to see ducks there, splashing in a pond. Brenner is indignant. What hypocrisy, since Mauriac liked to eat duck.

I have not quoted from Jacques Brenner's book to ridicule its author. I am close to thinking he is right. After all, one is entitled to know if the writers one admires were agreeable or disagreeable people, and knowing their attitude toward animals is not a bad criterion.

All of them give themselves away when they speak of dogs, revealing, rather, their own nature. Octave Mirbeau, for example, published a rather thick book entitled *Dingo,* devoted to the exploits of an animal that goes by that name, an Australian dingo, a liminal beast—part dog, part wolf. The author's misadventures on account of this companion are only a pretext for his bitter portrait of human depravity and meanness, both in the city and in the countryside. Dingo is a perfectly subversive animal. He slaughters other animals, is antimilitarist, attacks anything wearing a uniform, and shows affection only for paupers, vagrants, a tubercular actress, and even a pedophile murderer. Dingo's crimes and bad company secretly delight his master, who thinks all of us harbor a criminal aspect within ourselves. Dingo allows Mirbeau to spit out his own meanness and his contempt for his fellow citizens. One of the most grotesque characters in his book is a vet who thinks that rabies does not exist:

> "And the Pasteur Institute?"
>
> "A joke—they treat rabies because they invented it and they don't want to go bankrupt. The Pasteur Institute decided that dogs should have rabies, the way governments decided that people need religion."

Octave Mirbeau's poor opinion of the human race contaminates his feelings toward dogs: "The crime, the unpardonable crime, of human friendships is that our painful experience of them also makes us doubt the impartiality of dogs."

Dingo himself, at heart, isn't mean. He is a rather ingenious killer, driven by an ancestral instinct. The true sadist is his little companion Miche, a young cat that plays for hours at torturing the birds she catches instead of killing them straight off.

"What are you writing right now?" I am often asked. "A novel? Short stories?"

I say I'm writing this book about, among other things, dogs in literature. I might even call it *Doggone Literature*. A fatal mistake! Since then, everyone has been urging me not to forget: "Remember, that dog on page 179 of the novel I published twelve years ago? I hope you're going to talk about him."

That remains to be seen. The longer I write, the more I think of my book about dogs as an assembly of people I like. I don't want to invite the rest. Wagner may well try to touch our hearts by describing the loss of his Great Dane, and Céline may tell us about the death of his dog Bessy—we have nothing in common.

My publishing house is welcoming to dogs, whether those of its authors or those of the people who work there. Claude Gallimard's cocker spaniel Harry never left his office. Harry was very friendly to us and to authors—with one notable exception. The moment he saw Aragon, he wanted to devour him. You can imagine how this attitude, which has never been explained, mortified his master.

Animal-Machines

The seventeenth century was divided into two camps, not with respect to Descartes' philosophy as a whole, but on one particular point of his doctrine, which I mentioned in the previous chapter. Malebranche used to kick his dog in the name of animal-machines. Madame de Sévigné put Descartes and his theory in their place: "machines that love, machines that make a choice for someone, machines that are jealous, machines that are fearful." And she added, in a moment of indulgence, "Never would Descartes have meant us to believe it."

Once again, we must agree with the popular notion that Madame de Sévigné was more appealing than Madame de Grignan, her daughter. On December 17, 1690, Françoise Marguerite de Grignan wrote to her cousin Coulanges, asking her not to bring a dog to her daughter Pauline, who was sixteen years old at the time:

> We only want to love reasonable creatures here, those belonging to our own sect; we do not want to burden ourselves with *machines* of that sort. If they were constituted so that they had no dirty needs, well and good, but what they force us to put up with makes them intolerable.

Did Descartes merit such a "sectarian" disciple?

La Fontaine takes sides against Descartes, and the Cardinal of Retz endorses La Fontaine.

In the eighteenth century, Voltaire joins the ranks of the anti-Cartesians. Kant, in his *Critique of Teleological Judgment,* sends in reinforcements:

> From the similar mode of operation on the part of the lower animals, the source of which we are unable directly to perceive, compared with that of man, of which we are immediately conscious, we may quite correctly infer, on the strength of the analogy, that the lower animals, like man, act according to representations, and are not machines, as Descartes contends, and that, despite their specific difference, they are living beings and as such generally kindred to man.

Thus Emmanuel Kant liquidates Descartes in a single footnote. But the main argument advanced by the eighteenth century against the theory of animal-machines—by Jeremy Bentham, for example—is that animals experience suffering just as much as we do.

The Princess Palatine, Louis XIV's sister-in-law, comes to mind. She thought dogs had an immortal soul. She rejoiced at the idea that she would find in the next world not only her parents and friends but all the little creatures she had loved.

While certain thinkers denied animals the least degree of understanding, Racine, in *The Litigants,* staged a satiric and burlesque trial of the dog Citron, accused of having eaten a capon. Moreover, from the Middle Ages to the Renaissance and even later, many trials of dogs, pigs, and rats actually took place, according to due process. These trials often ended with death sentences, more rarely with acquittals.

The Litigants was inspired by Aristophanes' *Wasps,* which portrays the judgment of the dog Brigand, accused of devouring a cheese from Sicily. When I was in high school in the eighth or ninth grade, students were kicked out for reading

The Wasps. We can scarcely believe that today. It is true that Aristophanes' dialogue is crude in the extreme and that old Philokleon invites a female flutist to masturbate and fellate him. But these days, when people keep saying that reading is in so much trouble, we would be congratulating those precocious readers.

Modestine

May I allow myself a digression? I have to stigmatize Robert Louis Stevenson, the cruel author of *Travels with a Donkey in the Cévennes*. Here, indignation compels me to leave my subject matter and leap, for a moment, from dog to donkey. Poor Modestine! When the Scottish traveler complains that his arm aches from striking her on the spine with his switch, he listens to an innkeeper who tells him, "Such a beast as that feels nothing." Then he arms himself with a pin. What bliss: "no more flailing with an aching arm . . . , a discreet and gentlemanly fence. And what although now and then a drop of blood should appear on Modestine's mouse-colored wedge-like rump?" Arriving at Saint-Jean-du-Gard, Modestine can go no farther. What does Stevenson do? "Being in a civilized country of stage-coaches, I determined to sell my lady-friend and be off by the diligence that afternoon."

Hadn't Stevenson read *Tristram Shandy*, especially chapter 32 of book 7, so full of love and compassion:

> Now, 'tis an animal (be in what hurry I may) I cannot bear to strike—there is a patient endurance of sufferings, wrote so unaffectedly in his looks and carriage, which pleads so mightily for him, that it always disarms me; and to that degree, that I do not like to speak unkindly to him: on the contrary, meet him where I

will—whether in town or country—in cart or under panniers—whether in liberty or bondage—I have ever something civil to say to him on my part; and as one word begets another (if he has as little to do as I)—I generally fall into conversation with him; and surely never in my imagination so busy as in framing his responses from the etchings of his countenance—and where those carry me not deep enough—in flying from my own heart into his, and seeing what is natural for an ass to think—as well as a man, upon the occasion.

Since I'm handing out grades, I should say a word about Thomas Mann. I'll leave aside *Tobias Mindernickel*, in which a humiliated man takes revenge on his dog, going so far as to kill it. Mann also devoted a long text, *A Man and His Dog*, to an appealing mutt named Bashan. What a sense of superiority! What condescension! Bashan's unreserved affection for his master is held at bay by Thomas Mann. Though calling him "a fine fellow," he regards the dog as having "no sense of honor, no strictness with himself." Whenever necessary, he sets him straight with a beating. Bashan then starts to howl. This is because he is "coarser-fibred . . . like the lower classes; but like them also he is not above complaining." It would be hard to find pages more turgid than these, which aspire to take their place among the classics of animal literature, and which their author has dubbed "an idyll."

Gaston Febus

Nature lovers such as Maurice Genevois write wonderfully about animals, both the kind that roam free and the kind that live with humans. Like Francis Jammes, however, they are often hunters. They agree to spill the blood of animals. And although they understand the behavior and character of dogs better than others, they cannot help but consider them from too functional a point of view. When all is said and done, the hunting dog, the herd dog, the sled dog, the avalanche dog, and the police dog have negligible utility compared to that of a dog with no specific purpose. A dog of this kind is meant to give and receive friendship and love.

The grandfather of hunter-writers is Gaston Febus de Foix-Béarn. His *Book of the Hunt,* begun in 1387, is a natural history, a manual of veterinary art, an encyclopedia of hunting, as well as a work of literature that includes anecdotes, tales, recollections. Febus tells the famous story of Aubri de Mondidier's faithful greyhound: this animal unmasked his master's assassin so successfully that King Charles V ordered a trial by combat to decide between the dog and the accused killer. In the ensuing duel, the dog emerged victorious and the man was condemned to death. Gaston Febus spoke Gascon dialect, but he wrote in French, albeit with apologies:

The dog is loyal to its master and with good and true love. The dog is of good understanding and great knowledge and great judgment. The dog has force and goodness. The dog has wisdom and is a true beast. The dog has a great memory. The dog has a great sense of smell. The dog has great diligence and great power. The dog has great valor and great subtlety. The dog has great lightness and great perception. The dog is good for giving orders to, since it learns everything just as a man does when taught. Much frolicking is in a dog. So good are dogs that rare is the man who doesn't want to have one, either for one job or for another.

Of course, I had never heard of this passage when as a child, I used to walk with my dog Dick past the statue of Gaston Febus at Henri IV's castle in Pau. I knew of Febus only as the medieval sovereign who had imprisoned his son and slaughtered him by his own hand.

A few decades after Gaston Febus's *Book of the Hunt* was written, Charles d'Orléans paid tribute to his "Briquet with the floppy ears." He went farther than that, devoting one of his ballads to his Briquet grown old:

Old Briquet is resting
And no longer dares to work

Briquet doesn't even bark anymore. But he must be forgiven: "The old can do so little!" They'll let Baude, the new dog, beat the bushes. "Old Briquet is resting."

Novels of chivalry abound in one-on-one combats between valiant knights and dogs as huge as they are ferocious. The most famous is the one waged by Tirant le Blanc with a mastiff even bigger than he, belonging to the Prince of Wales. In the end, after a combat whose outcome is long uncertain, the knight bites the dog on the neck and manages to choke it. Cervantes cites this exploit in chapter 6 of the first part of his *Don Quixote.*

In antiquity, Aristotle achieved a feat of scholarship with his *History of Animals.* The minuteness of his observations and the extent of his knowledge concerning the animal kingdom are astonishing. Here, for example, are a few lines about dogs:

> Males generally begin to raise a leg to urinate at the age of six months. Some do not do so until they are eight months old, and still others do it even before they are six months old. In other words, they do this as soon as they reach puberty. Females always squat to urinate, though they are occasionally seen raising a leg for this purpose.

In an age rich in wonders, the *Fioretti* attribute to Saint Francis the absurd exploit of having turned the wolf of Gubbio into a vegetarian. As if this could make a wolf happy! The literary posterity of Gaston Febus and Saint Francis includes those who try to speak of animals as they really are, and those who practice anthropomorphism and generally make fools of themselves. Alphonse de Toussenel (1803–1885), with his "passionate zoology," opined that the cuckoo "seems to choose its victims from the most interesting families." Spoken like a society matron.

There was a time when Jules Romains was admired because, in *Men of Good Will,* he delivered the interior monologues of the student Jerphanion, the assassin Quinette, the Abbé Jeanne, and the dog Macaire in exactly the same tone. It was a triumph at once of psychology, of social portraiture, and of history. Few readers were troubled by the fact that these well-meaning characters, both the two- and the four-legged ones, all sounded like Jules Romains.

Worst of all is a writer who makes animals talk, as Colette does in her *Creature Conversations.* Anyone trying to write like a dumb animal writes like a dumb animal.* I must admit, how-

---

*A play on Pascal's famous dictum, "Anyone who tries to act like an angel is acting like a beast" ("Qui veut faire l'ange fait la bête").—Trans.

ever, that there is a lovely passage in *Claudine in Paris,* describing a cat squatting in her litter box. Colette should have paid attention to Rivarol (whom I've already cited): "The expressive looks and sounds made by a dog are only the signs of some momentary affection, and not an extensive dealing in ideas; they make for very short monologues."

Rivarol's amazing intuitions anticipated Pavlov's studies by a good hundred years. The theory on conditioned reflexes dates from 1903, but Rivarol, as early as 1797, wrote that "any sound that reaches animals at the moment when their food arrives is associated with it."

Let us ignore the descriptive conceits of Jules Renard, in his very unnatural *Natural Histories.* Monkeys are "bad boys who've torn the seat of their pants!"

Two Hunters

Turgenev is well known for his *Memoirs of a Hunter*. But he was also the author of a short story that has nothing to do with hunting; it is about the love between a man and a dog, and it continues to bring tears to many eyes. Turgenev wrote "Mumu" in prison in 1852, when he was locked up for a month in St. Petersburg for his obituary of Gogol. He was then exiled to his estates. The short story appeared in 1854 in the literary magazine *Sovremennik*, and the censor who passed it received a reprimand. The deputy minister of education wrote to the chief censor:

> The sensitive subject of this short story, and even more the tone used to describe the total dependence of serfs in face of the arbitrary whims of their mistress, can easily lead readers from the lower classes to condemn the relations that exist in our country between serfs and their owners, relations which, inasmuch as they are a national institution, must not be subject to one individual's judgment.

"Mumu" is a story about the serf Gerasim, employed as a yard porter in the Moscow palace of a nasty, capricious old woman. Gerasim is a giant and also a deaf-mute, isolated by his disability. He clings timidly to Tatyana, a poor laundress. But the mistress orders Tatyana to be married to a drunken shoemaker. Gerasim finds a consolation in adopting a little dog. He manages to name her by stammering two syllables "Mu-mu." After a year of love between the yard porter and his dog, the mistress gives an order for Mumu to be done away with. Gerasim is to drown her himself.

Faulkner too was a hunter. But I know of no author who writes about dogs as well as he does, with as much intelligence, love, and humor. In *Sartoris* I think there are as many dogs as there are human characters, and as varied. Old, young, wise, idiotic, not to mention a fox, Ellen, and her bastard progeny, losers from the start. The chapter in which a despairing Bayard Sartoris takes refuge at the MacCallums on Christmas Eve, along with their whole canine population, attains a level of humor and emotion that has never been equaled.

The Brutes

Louis Pergaud, though he barely avoids melodrama when describing the misery of a dog no longer wanted, or the torment of a magpie turned into an alcoholic by the regulars at a neighborhood bar, never stumbles into that anthropomorphism which is the worst danger when one is speaking of animals in general and of dogs in particular, the kind of nonsense of which there are innumerable examples. He uses misfortune of animals only to demonstrate human malice.

One of Chekhov's early stories, "A Pricey Dog," encapsulates all of human ignominy in three pages. A lieutenant is trying to sell his dog to another military man. Both are tipsy. The officer starts by singing the praises of his dog. He will not give it up for less than two hundred rubles. As the conversation goes on, he lowers his price. He finally offers the dog for nothing. And since his comrade is clearly not going to buy, this "dirty beast" will end up at the knacker's. She's actually a bitch, a "mongrel crossed with a pig."

In "Labyrinth," Louis Guilloux portrays a magistrate who one day finds himself suspected of being too interested in little girls. His colleagues then treat him in such a way that he has no choice but to hang himself. But he is remembered for another crime by the people who have passed through his court. To have some fun with his friends, he once got a dog so drunk that it died.

Human perversity is also denounced by Romain Gary in his *White Dog*. The author takes in a lost German shepherd in California. He quickly discovers that it is a "white dog," which means it has been trained to attack blacks. A trainer, affiliated with the Black Muslims, retrains him to his own liking. Soon the dog will be jumping at the throats of whites. We should mention, since it is so unusual, the way Gary speaks of animals and relationships with them. The snake in his novel *Big Squeeze* goes even farther than Flaubert's python in *Salammbô*. Such an extreme case of life with an animal companion is a funny way of describing solitude and the need for love—funny enough to make you cry.

In France's fair country, people don't have white dogs, but in their hatred for their fellow humans they have quickly adopted pit bulls and rottweilers, bred to attack anything that moves.

To the East

The pernicious training of the "white dog" makes me think of what Lena Zonina, Sartre's Russian translator, told me one night when the conversation got around to dogs. "We can't love them," she declared. "For us they are primarily the animals that guard the camps."

In Russia and its satellites, in the days of communism, the companion dog had a bad reputation; it was seen as a superfluous consumer and as a sign of individualism, selfish introversion. Having a dog was like turning one's back on the collective. I saw this in Czechoslovakia. Back in the early twentieth century, we should recall, Hašek's comic hero Schweik was a merchant and occasionally a dog thief. The communist authorities may have facilitated a similar activity. When they nationalized business, they forgot about the trade in dogs, which consequently began to proliferate. The state's response to this black market was to unleash repressive measures against the canine race. First a heavy fine, then the rounding up of any animal not on a leash. Milan Kundera describes the operation in *Farewell Waltz*. You see old men, pensioners with red armbands, carrying long poles equipped with wire loops at the tip, clumsily trying to catch dogs in the public gardens:

The old men armed with long poles merged in his mind with prison guards, examining magistrates, and informers who spied on neighbors to see if they talked politics while shopping. What drove such people to their sinister occupations? Spite? Certainly, but also the desire for order. . . . The desire for order is the virtuous pretext by which man's hatred for man justifies its crimes.

(Unfortunately, dogs also like order and detest anything that appears abnormal, irregular—which makes them suitable for guarding camps and other police duties).

As Jakub, one of the characters in Kundera's book, is trying to save a dog from being caught, a pretty young woman does all she can to prevent its rescue. This hurts even more than the laughter of the old men when they manage to snare an unfortunate mutt:

That young woman was his eternal defeat. She was pretty, and she had appeared on the scene not as a persecutor but as a spectator who, fascinated by the spectacle, identified with the persecutors. . . . Because to hunt men in our century is to hunt the privileged: those who read books or own a dog.

During the period of this repression against dogs, I was walking mine in the streets of Prague when a young man cried out, "Long live the dogs!" Old people came up to me and explained, in the French they had once learned, that life in the old days in their country was happier for dogs. It was their way of saying what they thought. Dogs were not allowed in restaurants. Still, one night, they let us in. And, even though there wasn't much to eat, the head waiter brought a plate of meat for Ulysses and set it conspicuously on the ground, right in the middle of the restaurant.

The Island of Oxias

Dog persecutions in communist countries were nothing compared to what once went on in Turkey. The illustrator and writer Sem provides an eyewitness account. The streets of Constantinople were famous for their population of gentle, sociable dogs. Pierre Loti, a French writer and naval officer, tells how much he liked them. There were thousands of Turkish dogs. In 1910, the police decided to eliminate them. They were not killed. They were deported to Oxias Island, a desert island in the Sea of Marmara. Under the blazing sun, without food or water.

Sem saw the dogs being rounded up by the Kurds, who attached them to enormous iron rods. They threw them, "panting like simple Armenians," into a cart hitched to oxen. Wagons loaded with cages regularly brought new victims to the island. You could smell Oxias from far away. Thousands of dogs and birds fought over the carcasses. They fought all the way to the water where corpses were floating. Many drowned.

This is what people did to dogs while waiting to apply the same methods to one another.

Enemies

Unlike many authors who drift into anthropomorphism, Pierre Gascar insists on the radical gap between humans and beasts. He widens that gap, showing each species locked in its solitude. Including humankind. In Gascar's work, even the dog becomes an enemy of man. In "The Dogs," one of the stories in his *Beasts and Men,* military dogs are as fiercely conditioned as Romain Gary's white dog. They are, literally, weapons of war. Gascar's entire book consists of recollections of wartime. Soldiers are reduced to little more than a lamentable herd. They meet up or cross paths with other herds: horses dying of hunger, rats preparing their great invasions. From visions of slaughterhouses emerges "the truth about this desolate world." It is a "sort of family party where there [is] no alternative but to drink deep of the wine of abomination. . . . At any moment, the beast's nature can change: we are at the frontier. The horse can be mad, the sheep rabid, the rat cunning, the bear ruthless: secondary states which give us a glimpse into an animal hell, and in which we recognize, with an astonished sense of kinship, our own tortured likeness, as in a scratched mirror."

A 1929 decision of the French Court of Appeals defines as dangerous any dog that "throws itself spontaneously at people in order to bite them."

Evolution

Birds are descended from reptiles, which is difficult to imagine for anyone who isn't a scientist. More surprising, whales and dolphins—according to the scientist Anne Collet—appear to be descendants of a kind of big wolf, the mesonyx, which lived in the Eocene epoch and then, following the inverse path of evolution, decided to return to the sea.

Our dogs come from human manipulations in breeding the wolf. From the minuscule Yorkshire to the huge German mastiff, all dogs are wolves. It is claimed—and I certainly believe it—that the natural behavior of domestic animals is practically identical to that of their wild ancestors. The only difference is the impact made on them by humans.

If a wolf cub less than six weeks old is brought up by humans, it will behave exactly like a dog. A puppy maintained without human contact in the first three months of life will remain completely wild, untamable.

Questions of Vocabulary

Next to a name such as Shangri-la or Home Sweet Home, garden gates often bear a sign "Beware of the dog." Never "Beware of people," though this may well be more apt.

The dog, often the object of excessive love, also attracts suspicion, disdain, and hatred—if we are to believe the way language uses its name. The moralist Chamfort's comment that "the natural character of the Frenchman is a mixture of monkey and bird dog" is not intended as a compliment.

"Am I a dog, that you come to me with sticks?" Goliath asked David. Since antiquity, in Greek as in Latin, calling someone a dog is a major insult. Although Ulysses wept on his return to Ithaca when he saw his poor old dog Argos, he was soon calling Penelope's suitors "dogs." Shakespeare's Julius Caesar, when Metellus demands the return of his brother from exile, replies that he will not be softened by "base spaniel fawning." Don't insist, says Caesar, or "I spurn thee like a cur out of my way."

You're a dog in the manger, we say. He's top dog. Flaubert "jabs a dog" at his house in Croisset—in other words, takes a nap during the day, without getting undressed or going to bed.

An unattractive woman is called a dog, a mean one a bitch. For the Romans, *caninae nuptiae* were shameless wedding nights. Horace calls the Furies *canes infernae,* dogs of hell. An unhappy life is a dog's life; one dies like a dog. The French word for riffraff is *canaille* (from *canis*). "Dog days" are unbearably hot. At a French police station, the sergeant at the front desk used to be known as the commissioner's dog. The crowning horror, in a famous speech in Racine's *Athalie,* is the image of devouring dogs fighting over pieces of Jezebel's flesh. The Greeks had a word *kunosparaktos,* meaning "torn apart by dogs."

The word *cynical* does not come from the crude manners of the adepts of Cynicism or from the fact that the Cynics considered themselves good guardians of philosophical principles. It's simply that Antisthenes, the founder of the school, gave his speeches in a gymnasium called the Cynosarges (the White Dog). Besides which, he referred to himself as "a real dog." As for Diogenes, his true mascot was not a dog but a mouse stripped bare. Yet legend shows him identifying more often with a dog. According to one version of his death, it was caused by a bite on his foot, incurred while he was arguing with some dogs over a piece of octopus. Hipparchia, one of the rare women in the history of philosophy, formed a cynical couple with Crates, sleeping anywhere or coupling in public.

The positive meanings for dog are equally strange, although they often involve a hint of irony and ambiguity:

> And I will finally know the heaven
> Of being called my dog, my little radish

writes Auguste Vacquerie in jest.

Masochistic and proud, Aragon's hero in *Irene's Cunt* proclaims, "I was her dog. That's my way."

Jacques Brel goes even farther: in the song "Don't Leave Me" he says, "I will be the shadow of your dog."

Why do we say about an attractive woman, in French, "elle a du chien"—she's got dog? In Aristide Bruant's song, a girl is so nice and sweet, "with an odor of red hair that sends shivers," that she's called "Nini-dog-skin." In the most X-rated passage in Céline's *Death on the Installment Plan,* Louison cries out to young Ferdinand, "Bite, pretty little dog…Bite into it!"

Humans and dogs have been living together for some twelve thousand years, and this is what human language has come up with. Along with the letter *r,* which the Romans called *canina littera,* because it sounds like a growl.

A Dog's Heart

In life, people often hide behind their pets, using them as a screen between themselves and others. In literature, too, animals often serve as a cover for discussing human passions. Unlike anthropomorphism, which is a naive interpretation of animal mentality, this use of human language in animals' mouths is a deliberate device. La Fontaine employed it. So did Kipling, twice over, by making Mowgli a little man raised by animals, albeit animals that think like people. Nor can we forget the stoic words of Vigny's dying wolf.

Fable sometimes becomes political, as in George Orwell's *Animal Farm*, with its now proverbial "All animals are equal but some animals are more equal than others." Mikhail Bulgakov, in *Heart of a Dog*, goes even farther and creates a hybrid. A scientist grafts the pituitary and genital glands of a proletarian onto a dog. This creature becomes a perfect scum, gets himself named director of the subsection in charge of purges in the city of Moscow, and denounces the professor who transformed him into a man. Not until the disastrous grafts are removed from him does he become a good dog again, remembering his Newfoundland ancestors.

Fantasy literature in general makes good use of the animal kingdom. In Vassili Aksyonov's *Moscow Saga*, a very friendly German shepherd called Pythagorus by his masters (though he thinks of them not as his masters but as his father, mother, brothers, and sister), remembers having once been the young prince Andrei de Polotsk, one of the victors in the battle against the Tartars at Koulikovo in 1380. One day he finds himself face to face with a squirrel, and the little rodent's glance is that of a young Finnish girl in a linen dress he had met at Derpt during the first campaign at Livonia.

In one of Supervielle's finest tales, "The Woman Found," a man who died in a shipwreck grows bored in the underworld and agrees to inhabit the body of a fox terrier so as to see his wife again. It doesn't do him much good. In another case, Supervielle devotes a tale to Cerberus, the dog from hell—indeed a pack of dogs since he has three heads. Cerberus is disappointed when he sees his sister, the Hydra from Lerna who was killed by Hercules. Pluto, however, consoles him: "What do you want, my little pack, you have to make the best of it; a sister, a spouse, or a mother is never exactly what one expected."

Dogs and the few other animals in Kafka are, in general, merely metaphors for our behavior and our condition—for example, the incorrigible guard dog that keeps running away, abandoning its post. Except for their names, there is nothing doglike about these dogs. In his complex and enigmatic "Investigations of a Dog," Kafka gives voice to an animal that meditates on music, on the earth and its nourishment, on the impossibility of achieving communal life, on liberty, even on theology and religion. A philosopher dog that seeks out the truth while mistrusting it. The profound song of a hunting dog carries our hero beyond himself, in an experience that cannot be communicated—no doubt that of death. In *The Trial*, Joseph K. dies, in his own last words, "Like a dog!"

Cervantes, in "The Dialogue of Dogs," also turns dogs into philosophers. Showing a very modern sense of humor, the dog Berganza is not too surprised that he can speak, but he finds it strange that his fellow creature Scipion knows Greek etymologies. In the nineteenth century, E. T. A. Hoffmann borrowed Berganza from his old colleague Cervantes to write "An Account of the Latest Fortunes of the Dog Berganza."

And let us not forget Daniel Pennac and Julius, Malaussene's dog, with its terrible stink, though we may still remember him both as a pooch and an echo of Dostoyevsky's Prince Myshkin.

Dreams after Ulysses' Death

Dogs do speak. They speak to us in our dreams. I have met many men and women who, like me, dream about the dog they loved who is no more. They rediscover him at night, many years later, not exactly as he was but lending himself to the distortions and cruel fantasies of dreamwork. So they can't always expect happy reunions. Sometimes Ulysses, my alter ego, my double, doesn't recognize me or pretends to ignore me, which fills me with distress.

A dog called Orestes, a key figure in J.-B. Pontalis's *Far,* appears to the narrator in a dream. When the narrator promises to take him out soon, Orestes responds, articulating each word: "I do not believe you." Pontalis notes in passing, "Why do we call them dreams when no reality is ever as true?

I AM TAKING a walk with Ulysses on a small square; at one end is a synagogue, its large doors wide open. There are many people on the square. Along the street that borders it, on the side opposite the synagogue, trestles are being set up, and on each trestle is a sewing machine. A lot of people start to sew, and the Jewish neighborhood hums with activity. I lose sight of Ulysses in the crowd and tell myself I need to look for him. I walk across the square and soon catch sight of him. At that moment it starts to rain, harder and harder. People who have only just set up their sewing machine quickly take them down. I rejoin Ulysses and we try to leave, though the rain is now torrential. We seek refuge in a café at one corner of the square with the sign "Uncle Anghel."

I FIND ULYSSES in the midst of a group of people. I signal to him. He stops for a moment. I remind him that he lives with me, that we love each other. He agrees to give me a quick lick. Then off he goes with those other people. I wake up crying.

I NO LONGER CRY, but I dream that I am crying.

ONCE AGAIN, I AM LOOKING for Ulysses in a dream. He is lost. Suddenly, in a dark corridor, I see my own double appear, facing me. I feel terror, as if death were coming for me.

PEOPLE PRAISE DOGS' prodigious sense of smell and generally add that their sight is only mediocre. I am not so sure. One day, walking along the rue Saint-Dominique, I saw a man on the opposite sidewalk who looked a lot like me, my double. Ulysses noticed him. He too was struck by the resemblance. For a second he pulled at his leash. Then he remembered he was with me. He looked at the double, he looked at me. He was totally bewildered, just as we would be, in the grip of what Freud called "the uncanny."

TO STAY WITH THE FOUNDER of psychoanalysis, and to continue with the theme of abandonment, we know that Sigmund Freud loved dogs. He even translated Marie Bonaparte's *Topsy: The Story of a Golden-Haired Chow* into German with his daughter Anna. Freud's own last chow, a female, was called Lün. In his London office, transformed into an infirmary as he lay dying of jaw cancer, he wanted to see her. But Lün, terrified by the odor of the cancer, refused to go near him and cowered in a corner. According to the people closest to him, Freud was deeply saddened by this behavior. What other messenger could have made it so clear that he was no longer part of life, that he had just crossed over to death?

Flush

The first problem a novelist faces is point of view. Should one write in the third person, or use a narrator? Will the narrator be the hero, a secondary character, or merely a witness? Will the author be omniscient, like God?—a technique which, at least since Sartre criticized Mauriac for it, has been frowned upon. Must the story unfold through the eyes and the consciousness of a single person? It is important to get it right. Virginia Woolf found an original solution in *Flush*. The character she chose was a cocker spaniel.

The dog Flush is not without precursors, though in other animal species. There is Cadichon, the Countess of Ségur's donkey; Murr, Hoffmann's cat; and Natsume Soseki's hero, who has no name but proclaims arrogantly, "I am a cat." For Virginia Woolf, however, it was not a matter of fantasy. She always tried to connect fiction to biography. The subject of *Flush*, once removed, is the life of Elizabeth Barrett Browning. But we are aware of her life only through the biography of her dog, the aforementioned Flush. We will learn everything about Flush, about his feelings, his thoughts, and even his dreams.

Showing the life and loves of a woman through her dog amounts to what has since been called the "estrangement effect." As Marguerite Yourcenar points out, "the dog's perspective is like that of Sirius, the dog star. Just as a few drops of alcohol stirred into liquid lose their strength and all but disappear except for a slight mist, the drop of passion tends to dissolve over great expanses of time into poignant memories, hopes, vague desires, or confused obsessions, which ultimately transform themselves into poetry."

Virginia Woolf, of course, is also having fun. She parodies biographies, beginning with staggering etymological hypotheses—the Carthaginian and Basque languages are brought into play—and historical accounts of cocker spaniels. It's quite a while before our hero arrives at 50 Wimpole Street, the famous house where Elizabeth Barrett lived as a secluded invalid in her back bedroom.

Flush was not purchased. He was a present from the excellent Miss Mitford. Unlike my poor Dick, who was used to settle a debt, Flush "was of the rare order of objects that cannot be associated with money." Besides, social inequities did not escape Flush. They affect dogs as much as humans.

In an earlier chapter I spoke of the importance of odors for dogs—and for Flush in particular. When he enters 50 Wimpole Street, the Barretts' home is described—room by room, all the way back to the dark bedroom in which Elizabeth lives—not by what Flush sees but by what he smells. Later, to his despair, the room will be invaded by the odor of a certain Mr. Browning.

Likewise, when the Brownings set up household in Italy, we get an extraordinary description of Florence, not visual but conveyed uniquely through the odors of the streets on which Flush roams.

For the time being, on Wimpole Street, Flush does without sun, fresh air, or grass in order to live at the feet of his mistress in the shadows of her bedroom. Elizabeth expresses her gratitude, at least for the duration of a poem:

But of *thee* it shall be said,
This dog watched beside a bed

Day and night unweary,
Watched within a curtained room
Where no sunbeam brake the gloom
    Round the sick and dreary.

Roses, gathered for a vase,
In that chamber died apace,
    Beam and breeze resigning;
This dog only, waited on,
Knowing, that, when light is gone
Love remains for shining.

Love such as this demands reciprocity. But Elizabeth's love is highly narcissistic. She loves Flush because she thinks he looks like her. The dog's long ears and the heavy curls that framed the poet's long face did give them a slight family resemblance.

Elizabeth finds an accomplice in Flush. On the sly, he eats the chicken wings and rice pudding that Mr. Barrett has ordered to be served up to his anorexic daughter.

Communion has its limits. Elizabeth cannot grasp the centuries-old atavistic urges that lie dormant in Flush. And the dog does not understand why his mistress weeps hot tears, without the least external provocation from words or odors. It is the same when she writes. What happens when she writes? And the emotion that overwhelms her when she reads certain letters! Flush senses it even before she opens the envelope.

This failure of understanding is only the beginning. Then Robert Browning makes his entrance. Flush can't stand the intruder's yellow gloves. Now the once beloved dog is cast into a terrible loneliness.

The art of Virginia Woolf shows us the progression of the love affair between Elizabeth and Robert without the need for any dialogue, since Flush does not understand human speech. Changes in the modulation of voices are all he needs.

On July 8, 1846, unable to control himself any longer, Flush bites Mr. Browning through his immaculate trouser leg. Crowning his humiliation, the two lovers pay no attention to this aggression. Mr. Browning brushes off the dog with a flick of his hand, and they continue their conversation. But once the visitor has left, Elizabeth tells Flush that she will never love him again. And these words a dog understands.

Elizabeth does indeed become less affectionate. Flush gets one of his paws caught in the door of her four-wheeler, and he yelps. She laughs at him. She says he's exaggerating, that he is of the "Byronic School." Writing about the incident, she uses a French expression: "il se pose en victime"—he's acting like a victim.

Flush will not be Byronic for long. He finds himself brutally transformed into a character out of Dickens. He is stolen. Dog theft seems to be a special feature of London history. Even the dogs of kings and princes got stolen. Charles II, for example, had to publish a notice in the *Mercurius Politicus* in 1680, announcing the theft of his black dog. Flush was stolen three times, though Virginia Woolf condensed the three episodes into one, for the sake of unity. It cost his mistress a total of twenty pounds. Dog theft was like a tax. Saint Giles, the neighborhood next to Wimpole Street, stole what it could, and Wimpole Street paid what it had to. Those who didn't pay received a package containing the head and paws of their pet. The residents of both neighborhoods were aware of this custom. But poor Flush, thrown into a dark, putrid hovel in the company of other stolen animals, a den in Whitechapel where bandits shared their loot, has no idea what was going on. A sordid episode ensues, rich in plot twists. Elizabeth fights alone against everyone, since her father and Robert Browning, along with the rest of Wimpole Street, refuse to give in to the blackmailers. Too bad for Flush. Elizabeth ventures to the wretched hovel of the thieves' "Society." Since a writer wastes nothing, we find an evocation of these slums in her novel in verse, *Aurora Leigh*.

In making us understand everything through the limited understanding of a dog, Virginia Woolf continues to rise to the challenge she has set for herself. We infer the secret marriage of Elizabeth Barrett and Robert Browning in Marylebone Church because Flush notices his mistress leaving the house one morning without him, at an unusual hour, in the company of her chambermaid Lily Wilson, who is to be her witness.

The Brownings leave for Italy. It is through the novelties encountered by the aristocratic Flush that we understand the differences in mentality and customs between England and Italy. Taking off on his own from the Casa Guidi while Elizabeth is giving birth—yet another drama—Flush discovers that Italy is infested with fleas. Elizabeth Browning doesn't mince words: "Savonarola's martyrdom here in Florence is scarcely worse than Flush's in the summer."

Many years later, Scott and Zelda Fitzgerald described how "there were fleas on the gilded filigree of the Grand Hôtel in Rome; men from the British embassy scratched behind the palms; the clerks said it was the flea season."

Flush, transformed into a democrat and ready to mix with the riffraff, escapes into the streets of Florence, but not to go into churches and admire the frescoes. The *odor di femina*, the call of love, makes him run from one end of the city to the other.

This reminds me of my travels with Ulysses. Aside from the pleasure of his company, he was of great service in a country like Italy. He spared me the burdens of culture. Instead of going into museums and churches, I was the person who stayed at the door looking after the dog. The two of us settled ourselves on the steps. And sometimes we even fell asleep, happy as clams.

After a brief return to London with his masters, Flush goes back to Florence. He grows old. During this period, around 1854, Elizabeth and her contemporaries are caught up in a craze. They turn tables. They call up spirits. One afternoon when Elizabeth is lying on the sofa reading, a noise makes her look up. Is it a spirit? No, only poor Flush, who has lain down beside her to die.

Flush is buried in the vaults of Casa Guidi, Elizabeth in the Piazza Donatello, the English cemetery in Florence, Robert Browning in Westminster Abbey.

Repeatedly, Virginia Woolf draws us into the solitude of Flush, a mental isolation that recalls the condition to which Camus condemns his "stranger," the only difference lying in Flush's extreme sensitivity and emotion. One of the secrets of this novelist's art is to establish a dissonance between a character and the exterior world. She is the writer of solitude, or rather of solitudes: that of the subject and that of the object. She brings all things back to their singularity and to their isolation.

The Fiancée of Goering's Dog

I once had a dog I didn't deserve. A female Malinois, a variety of Belgian shepherd, which I had rashly decided to purchase from a kennel near the Porte d'Italie in July 1946, when I had no housing and was going from one borrowed apartment to another. Not satisfied with that, I got her married. Natasha, a journalist in Pierre Lazareff's entourage, was the wife of a general, one of the Free French, who had come home from the Syrian campaign with a wooden leg. He was not in the least a man-the-torpedoes, all-work-and-no-play military type. He reminded me more of Maurice Chevalier. He set up house in the Bois de Boulogne, in an architectural folly that had previously belonged to a duke. The interior imitated that of a ship. It was said that the duke had held orgies there, which he called "cruises." He would come home with a hangover and explain to the duchess that the sea had been rough. That is where I went to attend the marriage of my dog, whose name was Sarigue.

While in Germany, the general had made off with a superb German shepherd formerly the property of Hermann Goering. Sarigue was destined for no ordinary husband. But the general also possessed an enormous briard. Sarigue, hussy that she was, traitor to the good shepherd name, only had eyes for the briard. We had to hide the hairy creature so that the arranged marriage could take place.

A little earlier, in July 1947, I had entrusted Sarigue to Albert Camus, who had just rented a property in Choisel, in the Chevreuse Valley. I still have Camus's letter arranging the day he would pick up the dog. It bore this postscript: "She'll do just fine here. She'll have acres to explore." He took her on the Metro with him, the Sceaux line.

Camus soon grew tired of the country and returned to his apartment on the rue Séguier, leaving the property, along with Sarigue, to Jules Roy. This fellow, whom we always called Julius, kept one of Sarigue's puppies, which he called Caesar. I don't know if Caesar was a son by Goering's dog or the fruit of a union that took place in Choisel. In the country, Sarigue, who was often out hunting, became quite a courtesan and had several litters. They had to buy her a dog's chastity belt (the technical name of which, in French, is "mascot"—no doubt an allusion to Audran's operetta *La Mascotte*).

Nearly fifty years later, Jules Roy had the curious notion of publishing the letters he sent to a woman with whom he was in love at the time and who had had the poor idea of marrying an Englishman and going to live on the other side of the Channel. In most of these letters I encounter Sarigue, her son, and their innumerable misdeeds. They liked killing lambs. The local gendarmes intervened. Julius, who had never had an even disposition, was furious and finally gave Sarigue back to me.

As a belated tribute to Sarigue, I included her photo in the illustrated collection on Camus that I published for the Pléiade series. She is wading in a little stream in Choisel. It's a frosty, sunny day. The grass is white and crisp. A small pleasure for private consumption, a wink to myself. I don't think Camus would have minded.

On Pure Love

Few authors who write about domestic animals address the real problem: What are they doing here by our side? Colette Audry, in *Behind the Bathtub* (which I've already cited), is the only author I know who has faced up to this issue. What she says is so true, so insightful, that one keeps coming back to it:

> The central point about dogs is, quite simply, that *people keep them;* whether they are handsome or ugly, mongrel or thorough-bred is irrelevant. They keep them, and care for them, till they reach an advanced state of senility: mange-ridden, scabbed with eczema, half-paralyzed, cataracts in both eyes—not to mention that dreadful old-dog smell.

Audry recounts and analyzes this relationship, focusing on a female dog that is particularly difficult and even dangerous—so dangerous that at one point its owners have to decide whether or not to exercise their power of life and death. And they must make this decision after love has had time to become firmly anchored. Love? There too, Audry looks at things straight on, not hesitating to disrupt the most conventional ideas about human couples or families:

Of all creatures on earth it is the dog that man has chosen as the object of his purest, most disinterested love. We marry a wife or a husband out of love, yes, but also in order to build for the future, whatever that future may be, however much or little it may be worth. We have children as an assurance against that future, to carry on our particular struggle or enterprise, to make men and women of them and a better world for everyone. We create them so that one day we may give them their freedom, let them be truly themselves. At least, that is what we think. Love may seem our immediate motivation, an irresistible force, but it is (contrary to what we suppose) really nothing but a bonus, an extra. Between husband and wife it is sometimes no more than a point of departure, the initial spark which serves as a pretext for other interests; people often, as we know, outgrow their early passions. Marital love can, according to circumstance, work for either total unity or complete disruption. Now the dog's role is rather that of a lover or a mistress, but even a lover or a mistress introduces some emotion, rightly or wrongly, other than "pure love"; a lifetime's secret self-aggrandizement, for instance. Between two human beings there is no such thing as "pure love," *in vacuo;* but the whole aim and purpose of owning a dog is to love it and be loved by it. Even if you acquire it with some other end in mind, this is always what it comes back to in the long run; this is what man has, ultimately, molded the dog *for.*

Which the marquise de Sévigné has in mind when she writes, "There is no doubt that I aspired to the masterpiece of having but one dog."

Taking it upon herself to love a second dog at Les Rochers, while her own Marphise was far away in Paris, the marquise felt like a two-timer, unfaithful on account of "this perfumed little dog, extraordinarily beautiful, with ears, silky fur, sweet breath, sylphlike, and blond as blond can be," whose name—

what irony!—was Fidèle. True, while the good marquise couldn't find enough adjectives to praise him, all she fed him was bread.

D. H. Lawrence believes the dog has a double nature. On the one hand is a ferocious beast, made for the hunt, for pillaging, for blood. On the other, a creature possessed of a fatal need to love, which ultimately costs him his freedom, as Lawrence demonstrates in his short story "Rex": "We should not have loved Rex so much, and he should not have loved us." His conclusion—"Nothing is more fatal than the disaster of too much love"—coming, as it does, from the author of *Sons and Lovers*, applies not solely to the canine species.

The love that holds sway over the hearts of dogs as well as human hearts inspired Proust's "Letter to Reynaldo Hahn's Dog," written in child—or canine—language:

> My dear Zadig,
>
> I love you very much because you are soooo sad and full of love just like me; and you couldn't find anyone better in the whole world. But I am not jealous that he spends more time with you because that's fair and because you are sadder and more loving.

Intelligence, he explains to Zadig,

> is only useful for replacing the impressions that make you love and suffer by weaker facsimiles that make for less sorrow and give less tenderness. . . . Only when I've become a dog again, a poor Zadig like you, can I start to write, and it's only books written that way that I like.

It's an old literary device: in the seventeenth century, the *Mercure Galant* magazine published letters in verse written by the marquise Deshoulières's spaniel.

As for Reynaldo Hahn, he claimed his dachshund had such a fine ear for music that while he was composing his famous aria for *Ciboulette*, "Nous avons fait un beau voyage," the dog started to howl until Hahn transposed the entire piece to another key.

Misanthropes

Loving dogs goes along, more or less, with despairing of humans. Schopenhauer, the pessimist, wrote about the goodness of dogs: "I would have no pleasure living in a world where dogs did not exist." Depressed, and prey to phobias, he alternated portraits of dogs with portraits of great philosophers on the walls of his little apartment in Frankfurt.

Baudelaire's disappointments gave rise to extreme hatred and contempt for Belgians in general, which he expressed, rather extravagantly, in *Poor Belgium!* Only the dogs were appealing. Valiant too: they were hitched to carts, where they seemed content to rival horses.

He also saw a spectacle beyond commentary—"the man who gets rich at fairs by eating live dogs."

The dogs in Brussels had no gaiety.

The sadness of animals. The dogs get no more petting than the women. It is impossible to make them play and frisk. They are as surprised as a prostitute when you address her as "Mademoiselle."

Thomas Bernhard so abhorred humankind that he generalized his hatred to the dog, man's companion. In order to have a dog, he would have to allow someone into his house to look after it.

Inconceivable! Happily, since reaching adulthood, he always detested dogs: "I can't put up with either a dog or another person." We are close to Alphonse Allais's reasoning: fortunately I hate spinach, because if I didn't hate it, I would have to eat it, and since I hate it . . .

At the risk of contradicting myself, I'm enchanted by Thomas Bernhard's hatred of dogs. He is at the top of his form here. Schopenhauer, as I have mentioned, is known for his love of dogs. This is how our dog hater sees it:

> Even Schopenhauer was ruled in the end not by his head, but by his dog. This fact is more depressing than any other. Fundamentally it was not Schopenhauer's head that determined his thoughts, but Schopenhauer's dog. It was not Schopenhauer's head that hated the world, but Schopenhauer's dog. I don't have to be demented to assert that Schopenhauer had a dog on his shoulders and not a head.

Thomas Bernhard gets more and more carried away. Politicians love a dog and start wars that exterminate millions of humans. Then he falls back more modestly on an old family conflict:

> If you kept a dog at least! my sister said just before she left. It wasn't the first time. She's been saying it for years just to enrage me. A dog at least! I don't need one of course—I have my lovers, she said.

Living and walking with a dog actually reinforces your solitude, your distance from other humans. (Certain people, on the other hand, use their dog to start conversations with passersby and strangers, or to pick someone up.) When I was in the company of my dear Ulysses, I remember how often we exchanged a glance, signifying how annoying all the people around us were and how happy the two of us were to be together, facing the others, if not opposing them.

Roland Dubillard puts his finger on a question asked by all those who truly love dogs: "How is it that we are more satisfied by the understanding that can exist between a dog and ourselves than by that which exists between us and our fellow creatures?"

True misanthropes don't seek the company of dogs. A love of animals can also be the manifestation of an insatiable love of life. I don't think Picasso hated people. He had many friends. He adored women. But according to Brassaï, whose *Conversations with Picasso* are an authoritative source of information, animals were

> as indispensable at his side as a feminine presence. At the Bateau-Lavoir, he had three Siamese cats, a dog, a female monkey, and a tortoise; a tame white mouse lived in a table drawer. He liked Frédé's donkey, which grabbed a packet of his tobacco one day; loved the tame crow at the Lapin Agile and painted it— in *Woman with Crow*—with Frédé's daughter, who had become MacOrlan's wife. In Vallauris, he had a she-goat; in Cannes, a monkey. As for dogs . . .

Picasso bragged about having reflexes as quick as a dog. He owned two large hounds as well as a fox terrier, a dachshund, a Dalmatian, a boxer. They were named Elft, Frika, Loump, Yane. Kazbek, his Afghan hound, a little-known breed at the time, intrigued people. At the beginning of the Occupation, Picasso and Kazbek were accosted by a German officer. After this incident he ordered his chauffeur, Marcel, to respond to anyone who was curious: "It's a basset hound from the Charentes region."

Dog and Cat

André Gide had "the most neurotic dog imaginable." His name was Toby. In a diary entry of January 19, 1917, Gide notes a sexual deviation in this unfortunate animal, who enjoyed little success among bitches and not much more with an old cat, "who nonetheless excited him as much as a bitch, and who, for her part, provoked and pursued him as though he were a tomcat. It is hard to imagine behavior more absurd and shocking; Toby would wear himself out, going after her for hours and days on end."

Animal literature rarely unites two antagonistic types in this way. Humans can generally be divided into two camps: dog lovers and cat lovers, for rare are those who love all animals. One must be careful about entering into this quarrel. I will content myself, prudently, by adding one piece of evidence to the dossier. Herodotus, speaking of the animals of Egypt, remarked:

> In whoever's house a cat dies naturally, those who dwell in the house all shave their eyebrows, but only these; if the dead animal is a dog, they shave all their body and head.

The sage Herodotus seems to be recommending prudence in all that relates to passion for animals. He notices that in Egypt all animals are sacred, but he refrains from explaining why:

If I were to say why animals are declared sacred, my argument would lead me into talking of matters divine, and that is something I particularly shun.

Any bookstore will tell you that books about cats sell much better than books about dogs. Who's to say why?

The Night in Hendaye

One of the things about animal literature is that it stays with us from early childhood.

> Here is Bichonne
> Briquet's poor dog.

Are they still reading about Bichonne in primary school? In first grade, the title of my reader was *Jeannot and Jeannette*. Its descriptions and little stories portrayed a rural world where children wore clogs and where, it's fair to say, nothing was done to awaken a love for dogs. Dogs were mentioned only incidentally, as slaughterers of chickens, as eager to devour a sparrow fallen from its nest, even as infected with rabies—but happily Louis Pasteur, humanity's benefactor, could take care of that.

Despite the authority of that dog-unfriendly reader, who hasn't kept the four-legged heroes of many marvelous books close to their heart? How many generations of French schoolchildren came to love little Rémi and his faithful Capi in *Sans Famille*. I myself was crazy about *The Jungle Book*, from which our teacher read us an episode every year, right before vacation. And at the movies I wouldn't have missed the films starring Rin-Tin-Tin—the original, authentic Rin-Tin-Tin—for anything. In Pau, they played at the Olympia movie house, a place I never dreamed my parents would one day have the bizarre idea of buying and managing—a disastrous adventure that I attempted to resuscitate in a novel, renaming that wretched theater the Magic Palace.

Above all, I loved Jack London. Michael, the circus dog, was my favorite. His master, the leprous sailor, champion of the world of beer drinkers, also appealed to me greatly. In photographs of the Californian writer, you see a few of his companions: Brown Wolf, his son Glenn, Peggy the Irish terrier, in whose company on board the Minolta they were all nearly shipwrecked and eaten by natives of the Solomon Islands (an adventure that the author transposed to the dog Jerry, Michael's brother). Other photos show Jack London with horses, and even pigs.

Michael and Jerry weren't the only Jack London characters I appreciated. I liked the railroad hoboes, those hordes of unemployed who "rode the rails," crossing the United States on freight cars. And also Smoky Bellew and Shorty, those two great companions in the Great North. In my naïveté, I was surprised that in one episode Bellew could be in love with two women at the same time, the practical Joy Gastell and the romantic Labiskwee. But I'm getting away from my subject. Jack London is probably the only writer who has used the story of a dog as a vehicle for autobiography. I'm thinking of Buck, in *Call of the Wild:*

> There he lay for the remainder of the weary night, nursing his wrath and wounded pride. He could not understand what it all meant. What did they want with him, these strange men? Why were they keeping him pent up in this narrow crate?

Those are the reactions of Jack London himself when he was locked up in the Erie County penitentiary for vagrancy in Buffalo, in 1894.

My enjoyment of those books began at the orange cover, always bearing two strange names, those of the translators, eternally paired: Paul Gruyer and Louis Postif. To celebrate Jack London is to pay an old debt. I was thirteen. I was traveling with my father. We were on the way to Spain. We stopped for the night in Hendaye. It was hot. There were noises outside from a carnival. My father left me in the hotel room and went out with a friend who was along for the trip. I realized they wouldn't be home until very late. Alone, disoriented, I was in a state of distress that I still haven't forgotten. But I had a savior that night, a companion. It was Jack London and one of his books with the orange cover.

Michael, Jerry, White Fang, I knew they were fiction. That is why, despite all I owed them, they were one day supplanted by the sled dog Tempest, created by another writer of the Great North, Louis-Frédéric Rouquette, author of *The Great White Silence*. By a remarkable coincidence, I often saw the photo of a dog at the home of a friend of mine, never realizing that this friend was related to Louis-Frédéric Rouquette and that the dog was Tempest! We played music together, with Tempest lording it over us from his frame on the piano. Do people still read Rouquette, and what has happened to the photo of his dog? My friend, the pianist, was killed in the war.

Neither the years, nor what is usually called culture, the development of literary taste, have succeeded in chasing these two authors and their two- or four-legged characters from my personal pantheon.

I hoped my children would feel a similar camaraderie for a literary dog. So when they were eight and ten years old I read them a story by Chekhov, "Kachtanka," about yet another lost creature that becomes a circus dog and experiences much unhappiness before being reunited with its owners. It was a total flop, as they say in the theater. Even the name seemed silly to them.*

---

*"Kachtanka," pronounced in French, sounded to them like "cache ton cul," "hide your ass!"—Trans.

Debtors

With few exceptions, writers, as a breed, help themselves to animals more than actually helping them. In relations between humans and animals, it is always the human that is in debt. Take the rejects of humankind—drunk, stupid, or mean: no one wants to have anything to do with them except for some dog, which starts to follow just such a reject, to love and obey him. How many panhandlers use dogs to appeal to passersby, to obtain a handout more easily. Perhaps, when all is said and done, they too love their companions.

Dino, Queneau's Dog

Reading between the lines of discreet writers, you sometimes discover a secret relationship. Take Raymond Queneau. His short story "Dino" was about a trip to Portugal, which he described with extraordinary precision, managing to capture all of that country in six pages. He was accompanied on the trip by a dog called Dino. Dino was very good at fetching the stones his master threw for him, and knew how to beg for a lump of sugar or a piece of meat. And Queneau adds, quite simply, "The other regulars at the hotel looked at us, or rather looked at me since Dino did not exist."

This trip in the company of a dog that does not exist is the entire subject of the story. Which will not make Dino's disappearance, his infidelity, any less cruel.

You might wonder about all the references to dogs in Queneau's titles: *Oak and Dog, Dogweed, The Dog with a Mandolin.* In his rhymed version of a session of psychoanalysis, he wants to be both an oak—nobility and grandeur—and a dog—an animal that "devours and nips." A double blazon, the dialectic of sky and earth.

Queneau, as his exegetes have pointed out, is a diminutive of a word in the Norman dialect, *quen* or *quien,* dog, which is also found in the English word "kennel." "In Rouen, a small dog is called a *quenot,*" the *Dictionary of Conversation* assures us.

I don't want to stray from my subject, but in Japanese too the word for dog is *ken*, and one of the longest and best-known Japanese novels, written in the early nineteenth century, Bakin's *Naso Satomi Hakkenden*, tells the story of a dog promised the hand of a prince's daughter if the dog will save the prince from an enemy, followed by the story of eight knights incarnating the eight virtues of Confucius. In the name of each knight appears the character *ken*, dog.

To return to Raymond Queneau, I can testify that he refused a literary prize because his dog had just died, and he must surely have found it indecent that others intended to fête him at such a moment.

At the end of his life he took another companion, Taï-Taï, a female Tibetan terrier who never left his side. She was a very proud little character; she didn't like anyone to pick her up or cuddle her, and she responded with disdain to the signs of friendship shown by my great lump of a Ulysses (they occupied adjacent offices). I am sure that Raymond Queneau delayed going into the hospital because he didn't want to leave Taï-Taï, and that the delay hastened his death.

Horse, Goat, Dog

I left Caen, my native city, at the age of three. Which is to say I have hardly any memories of it. Three images, at most.

The horses harnessed to cabs parked along a square. It seems I got on well with one of the drivers, and he got along even better with the maid who took me for walks.

A goat by a canal, grabbing at my snack and devouring the paper it was wrapped in.

Finally, just before we moved away, a night scene: our dog Rita, true to her terrier nature, chasing a rat in a gutter.

Thus, from my early childhood, the only images that have survived are of animals: a horse, a goat, a dog.

The Dog-Book

And what if literature were a dog tagging along beside you night and day, a familiar and demanding animal that never leaves you in peace, that you must love, feed, take out? That you love and you hate. That hurts you by dying before you do, short as a book's life is, these days.

Translator's Note

The Difficulty of Being a Dog, among its many qualities, offers readers a charming survey of writing about dogs through the ages. In translating Roger Grenier's quotations from a wide variety of sources, I went to a number of published translations. Foremost among these was Robert Fagles' beautiful rendition of *The Odyssey* (New York: Viking Penguin, 1996), from which I drew the passage quoted in Grenier's preface, on the dog Argos. I have changed "Odysseus" to "Ulysses" for obvious reasons, and with Professor Fagles's gracious permission.

Appended to this note is an alphabetical list of translations I have used, in some cases with minor modification. Although some of these books are no longer in print, they are readily available through Web sites or public libraries, and together with the English-language texts Grenier discusses—classics like Virginia Woolf's *Flush* or Jack London's *Call of the Wild*— they make for a veritable reading course in canine literature. Where no appropriate English translation of a source exists, the translations are my own.

I could not have completed this project without the help and encouragement of Roger Grenier. For each writer he quotes, each text he describes, he was able to give me exact information about his source. Working together, we have expanded or edited certain passages with English-language readers in mind.

This translation benefited immeasurably from the critical and writerly talents of Arthur Phillips, who worked with me on an early draft. Margaret Mahan's superb copyediting helped transform Roger Grenier's elegant, understated French into the English it deserves. Alan Thomas, who acquired *The Difficulty of Being a Dog* for the University of Chicago Press, has contributed his wisdom about dogs and books all along the way.

Audry, Colette. *Behind the Bathtub: The Story of a French Dog,* translated by Peter Green, 47, 48, 51. Boston: Little, Brown, 1963. ("To Be Loved"; "On Pure Love")

Baudelaire, Charles. *Paris Spleen,* translated by Louise Varèse, 104, 105. New York: New Directions, 1947. ("Low Life"; translation modified)

Bernhard, Thomas. *Concrete,* translated by David McLintock, 52–53. New York: Knopf, 1984. Paperback edition, Chicago: University of Chicago Press, 1986. ("Misanthropes"; translation modified)

Brassaï, *Conversations with Picasso,* translated by Jane Marie Todd, 266. Chicago: University of Chicago Press, 1999. ("Misanthropes")

Cervantes, Miguel de. "The Dialogue of the Dogs," in *Exemplary Stories,* translated by Lesley Lipson, 250. Oxford: Oxford University Press, 1998. ("Fantasies, Symbols, Signals"; translation modified)

Chamfort, *Products of the Perfected Civilization: Selected Writings of Chamfort,* translated by W. S. Merwin, 189. Toronto: Macmillan, 1939. ("Questions of Vocabulary")

Gascar, Pierre. *Beasts and Men,* translated by Jean Stewart, 22, 49, 174. Boston: Little, Brown, 1956. ("Enemies")

Kafka, Franz. "Blumenfeld, an Elderly Bachelor," translated by Tania and James Stern, in *Franz Kafka: The Complete Stories,* 185. New York: Schocken Books, 1971. ("A dog, yes, but . . ."; translation modified)

Kundera, Milan. *Farewell Waltz*, translated by Aaron Asher, 101, 108, 109. New York: HarperCollins, 1998. ("To the East")

Maeterlinck, Maurice. *The Double Garden*, translated by Alexandre Teixeira de Mattos, 13. New York: Dodd, Mead & Co., 1904. ("The Difficulty of Being a Dog"; translation modified)

Mann, Thomas. "A Man and His Dog," in *Death in Venice and Seven Other Stories*, translated by H. T. Lowe-Porter, 235, 236. New York: Vintage Books, 1963 ("Modestine")

Meredith, James Creed. *Kant's Critique of Teleological Judgement*, 136. Oxford: Clarendon Press, 1928. ("Animal-Machines")

Rilke, Rainer Maria. Preface, translated by Richard Miller, to *Mitsou: Forty Images by Balthus*, 9. New York: Harry Abrams / Metropolitan Museum, 1984. ("A Reproachful Glance")

Sartre, Jean-Paul. *The Family Idiot*, translated by Carol Cosman, 1:137, 138. Chicago: University of Chicago Press, 1981. ("The Difficulty of Being a Dog")

Spinoza, Baruch. *Ethics Demonstrated in Geometrical Order*, translated by William Hale White, 4th ed., 155. London: Oxford University Press, 1930. ("Metaphysics"; translation modified)